What people are saying a

"This is a true and beautil... ... healing for two individuals whose paths crossed by what some would identify as an accident or bad luck. Little did either know that this horrible experience would be an opportunity for growth and a deeper understanding of faith. I totally recommend this book for those who believe that change is not possible for some individuals who have been perpetrators of crime, or for their victims."

– Pamela J. S. Rodden, PhD, LPC

"Rose Pauly offers a refreshing and challenging voice to our contemporary culture that seeks justice and retribution when confronted with criminal acts. Instead of simple platitudes about God's forgiveness, Rose takes us with her on her difficult journey to extend God's love to someone who had lost any sense of how to treat another human. But this book is unique in that we hear the other side of the story as well. The perpetrator gives us his perspective of the story as someone who was driven by his corrupted fantasies about women, to his time in the prison system, but most importantly how God was working in and through this darkness. Fear, obsession, violence, forgiveness, recovery, and grace are thoughtfully woven together in this engaging book."

– Dr. David P. Paris, Associate Director and Associate Professor
of New Testament at Fuller Theological Seminary,
author of *Reading the Bible With Giants*

"This story is riveting! Not only because of the gripping course of events but the profound ways God breaks in on some of the darkest days and seemingly hopeless circumstances."

– Aaron Stern, Pastor of Mill City Church,
Fort Collins, Colorado, author of *What's Your Secret?*

"I thought I had heard it all . . . until I read Rose Pauly's stunning story of *Desperate Hope*. The book's one-of-a-kind perspective of true events read like a thriller novel, which will inspire and awe the reader of God's perfect love."

— **Steve Merriman**, President of Tax and Accounting Firm

"Rose Pauly tells a riveting, inspiring true story of God's transcendent power breaking into daily human existence in a life-transforming, world-changing way. *Desperate Hope* is well worth your time and investment—a must-read!"

— **Rev. John C. Bangs**, DMin, Associate Professor of Ministry Leadership, Northwest University

"I have been privileged to know and mentor Matt for a number of years and can attest to the transformation in his life. *Desperate Hope* is the message of the gospel in a modern day, true story. It speaks of more than forgiving yourself and forgiving others. It's a riveting story that tells of the miracle of genuine reconciliation between victim and perpetrator."

— **Kent Hummel**, Lead Pastor Good Shepherd Church, Loveland, Colorado

"*Desperate Hope* is a powerful story of God's protection, redemption, and the transformative power of forgiveness. Here we see the gospel, which makes all things new, unfolding in the lives of both the victim and the perpetrator. The book moves me to live my life better. I highly recommend this book."

— **Kurt Fredrickson**, MDiv, DMin, PhD,
Associate Dean for Doctor of Ministry and
Assistant Professor of Pastoral Ministry
at Fuller Theological Seminary,
author of *That Their Work Will Be a Joy*

"Having known Rose for the duration of this story, I have been richly blessed by watching this redemption story unfold. *Desperate Hope* is a compelling example of how God's grace goes beyond salvation and forgiveness, including recovery, reconciliation, and restoration."

— **Clay Peck**, DMin, Lead Pastor of
Grace Place Church, Berthoud, Colorado

"Rose Pauly writes a gripping story of courage, compassion, and transformation, not only of her life, but of the man who tried to kill her. Every youth pastor, high school, and college student in America, no, the world, should read this testimonial. Through the power of Jesus Christ, it *is* possible to break *all* the bondages of Satan"

— **Debbie Martinez**, Missionary, School Administrator,
La Vega Christian School, Dominican Republic

"Few issues impact the well-being of our lives as much as fear and unforgiveness—both of which Rose Pauly has so powerfully addressed in her book. I was impacted by the hope and direction she offers in the retelling of her gripping, true story. This is a must-read."

— **David J. Niquette**, DMin,
Pastor Christ Center Community Church, Fort Collins, Colorado

Desperate Hope

DESPERATE

HOPE

An Unusual Journey to Freedom
from Addiction and Victimhood

ROSE PAULY

ETHAN HENRY

This book is dedicated to Steve,
Brent and Erica, Chris, and Ryan,
and to our first grandchild
whom we wait to meet with eager anticipation.

Contents

Preface

"Turn around and look up the street." The impression was subtle but real. Heading into my garage, arms loaded with books, I swung around and gazed up the nearly empty street. In the distance a man was getting out of his car. That wasn't so strange. Yet something gripped my heart with fear. Maybe it was the unexplainable shroud of darkness that appeared to be mysteriously framing his face. Maybe it was the way his gaze riveted on me, boring a hole in the pit of my stomach. Instinctively I headed for the gray button that would securely close the large garage door behind me, shutting me off from the imminent danger I felt was just yards away. Then another impression followed: "Turn around, go down your driveway and meet him." Nothing was making sense in this surreal moment. Without a second thought I complied with the strong directive that penetrated my mind with an unusual force. Little did I know what awaited me in the moments ahead. What followed changed the course of my life. I will never be the same.

Irrupt. The word now comes to life as if illuminated by a thousand candles. Its meaning once obscure to me has become a reality, a truth that has hit with its full force. *Irrupt* is the breaking in of something suddenly and without warning. It catches you off guard then leaves you changed. It is not the *erupt* of a volcano as it bursts outward with violent release. It is also not the *interrupt* of a small child as he tugs on his mother's sleeve, longing for a moment of her attention. *Irrupt* is something or someone entering abruptly, and from that moment on, everything is altered. It is something so unique and distinct that there is no other option than for the initial condition to be transformed. This is the story of an irruption, a dramatic and life-changing irruption, the irruption of lives that were on very different trajectories.

This story is not the usual one printed on the pages of the morning newspaper. It is not the customary message of a CNN broadcast. It is real and remarkable just because it doesn't fit the norm. This story has been over seventeen years in the making. It is about two lives, two very different lives, that intersected one day in a radical and dramatic way. It is a story of terror, shame, guilt, fear, darkness, hardships, prison, and hard work. But it is also the story of determination, celebration, restoration, and change. It is the story of growth, forgiveness, and recovery—recovery from addiction, pornography, bitterness, shame, and from the need to become a victim. And most important of all, it is the story of two people encountering God in a profound way.

While the events that took place in September of 1995 were unusual, the message flowing out of that time is one that speaks to every one of us. It is a message that meets our humanity at many different levels, touching upon our fears, identifying with our struggles, and acknowledging our weaknesses. Yet it also propels us to a new place of understanding and another way of being.

CHAPTER ONE

A Life-Changing Moment

The Intruder

Opening the shades, I looked out to see a gorgeous, sunny, fall Colorado day. It was the Tuesday following Labor Day weekend in September of 1995. It started out as any ordinary day with school lunches to make for my three small sons, a goodbye to my husband leaving for work, and books and notepads to be gathered for my morning classes at school. My mind was filled with the wonderful memory of the weekend we had just experienced. What a joy to spend time in the Colorado mountains, taking in the splashing stream of the Crystal River at Filoha Meadows, mountain biking along the rocky trails, shopping in the quaint and rustic stores of Redstone, and breathing in the mountain air. My father had discovered this remote location and booked a getaway for a family gathering knowing that we all needed the time away. As our three sons pedaled their small bikes on the trails, with cousins, grandparents, aunt, uncle, and father following behind, I looked up at the deep blue of the sky and knew that God was good. That afternoon when a colorful monarch butterfly decided to land on my head and ride out the journey parked in that place, I felt loved, content, secure, and filled with peace. Life was good, and there seemed to be reason to look to the future with anticipation. I had no idea that when I returned home after that wonderful weekend my life was going to be forever changed.

Trying to juggle a course schedule for a master of business administration from Colorado State University in addition to raising three sons was no easy task, but it was a challenge I was anxious to tackle. My husband had always been supportive of whatever endeavor I attempted, and this was no different. I guess he knew he was in for a wild ride when he married me. Classes flew by during the morning, and I finished in time to drop off the lunches to the boys and race home to complete errands and studying before it was time to travel the few miles back to their school for pickup. As I pulled into the driveway my mind was racing with the myriad of things I yet needed to do. Having just returned the night before from the three-day getaway, there was a house to clean, laundry to fold, phone calls to make, and studying to complete.

I took a deep breath, realizing that life in the fast lane had returned. I needed to stay focused on the duties at hand and the tasks to be accomplished. Parking in the driveway, I grabbed my books and was headed into the garage when something inside me caused me to turn around and look up my street. At the moment I felt a strange sense of apprehension that was inexplicable, yet real. There, some distance up the street, a man was getting out of his car and purposefully heading in my direction, his focus riveted on me. Though it was twelve o'clock noon there was full sun outside; I instinctively felt a darkness around him that was unmistakable. Instantly I knew I had something to fear. "Just get into the garage and close the door and pretend you never saw him," I thought. As I headed for the gray button on the wall, an impression came to me: "Turn around; go down your driveway to meet him. If you try to run now he will be in the garage with you by the time you close your garage door." It seemed prudent to follow the impression.

Turning around and heading down the driveway, I was met head on by the man fast approaching me with determination. As he came closer, fear began to mount. He was only a few yards away when I remembered him as someone I had met before. I quipped, "Hi, I didn't recognize you!" The darkness around him vanished, and there was an overwhelming rush of relief. He had come to our home about a year earlier looking for some work in construction. Since we needed cabinets built in the garage, he measured the space and gave us a bid. The bid was more than we were able to afford at the time, but we struck up a conversation, and he told us he was struggling to turn his life around. Since my husband and I were involved in promoting Christian music at the time, it seemed only natural to offer him some cassette tapes with music of encouragement and hope, which he readily accepted. The strange thing is, those cassettes had shown up back at our home about eight months later, even though no one ever remembered him dropping them off.

The recognition that took place that moment in the driveway caused me to drop the defenses and warnings that had weighed so heavy just moments before. "Hi!" he said. "I was just working on some cabinets at a neighbor's house. As I was driving by, I was thinking about those tapes you gave me. I really liked them and would like to buy some for myself. Could I get the titles from you?" Without a second thought I said, "Sure, come on in." I didn't want to lead him through the garage, so I went around the front of the house and guided him through the front door. I barely remembered noticing painters working on our neighbor's house.

He quietly shadowed me as I entered through the door. Oblivious to his demeanor, I began rattling off a one-sided conversation about being on vacation up in Redstone over the Labor Day holiday and trying to get things cleaned up after the long weekend. I directed him to the stereo where the cassettes were kept. I didn't notice that he had been following silently behind me. Chatting happily about our vacation, I took one of the tapes down from the shelf, remembering that it was the one I had given him before. "Here, I think that this . . ." At that moment he grabbed me from behind and thrust a knife to the front of my neck, its cold blade pressing against my throat. With his arms around me and the edge of the knife one move from severing my airway, he uttered into my ear, "Rose, don't struggle. Don't scream or resist. Just walk upstairs."

"This can't be real," I thought. Then the stark reality came crashing upon me like a body-crushing torrent. This was real. My heart immediately sank. I had been tricked and I was home alone.

Driven

Matt

I was a seven-year-old boy without direction. It was early in 1969, and I found it so hard to figure out what this life was all about. Yes, my family attended the local Catholic church, but I hated every moment of it. What was it they were saying during Mass? I couldn't understand any of it, and I didn't want to go there.

There were other things that captured my attention, like the tantalizing pictures I had recently encountered. While slipping away to a secret remote tree-fort, built by my second-grade friends, I couldn't help but stare wide-eyed at what I saw. Plastering the walls of this hideaway were full spreads of ladies like I had never seen before. I couldn't take my eyes off them. Looking back I realized this was hard-core pornography. I had never been exposed to it before, but I knew one thing—I was hooked. And from that day on, I looked for excuses to visit again. It was fodder for the fantasies that began at this young age. At the time it never occurred to me to wonder how eight-year-old boys acquired such a stash.

At twelve years old I went through confirmation, but it seemed more like a ritual than anything meaningful. I picked up the Bible and attempted to read the black and red words on the thin-leafed pages. It too made no sense to me. Why does everyone make such a big deal out of religion? It's just words on a page and empty voices in a cathedral. Isn't there more to life than this?

I still remember the day I saw some strange words in the Scriptures I held on my lap, a story in Genesis that I couldn't comprehend. Maybe my father could help me understand. He'd had a lot more experience in these things. I found my father in the other room watching TV and asked about the words I had read. Without taking his eyes from the screen my dad muttered something I couldn't hear. He seemed bothered by the intrusion and in his silent way let me know that I had offended him with my boorish question. I slipped away ashamed. Looking back I realize that we never went to church again from that day forward.

Not going to church was a great thing for me. I hated it anyway, and now I didn't have to deal with those monotonous hours. I was glad to be free. My parents were good to me and let me do most anything I wanted. God was not spoken of, and faith in a higher being was nonexistent. That was okay with me. Who needed it anyway? Soon I found myself not only uncomfortable around those who seemed religious but outright afraid of church people. They seemed so different. I couldn't relate nor did I want to, but something inside kept nagging as I entered into my teenage years. Was there a power greater than me? Was there something else out there that I could turn to in times of need? For some time I sought to find a place of significance in nature. Maybe this was the mystical and spiritual place where I could find comfort and peace, I thought. I seemed to feel God's presence in the mountains and beautiful scenery around me. However I soon lost interest, and cynicism set in. I felt like a loner trying to figure out God, but God was nowhere to be found. What made matters worse was that those who claimed to know him didn't appear to be any better off. "No one is right," I reasoned. "It's time to give up the pursuit." The end of my search had brought me to the only place that made sense. There was no God, and I felt comfortable letting the shallow dream go. Being an atheist was the only reasonable response, and I wanted to let reason drive me.

The problem was that reason was not what was driving me. I had been plagued by a fantasy world, a world that I had kept secret within me. As far back as I could remember, my mind had played tricks on me. The fantasies were often disturbing and involved sexual liaisons with helpless and defenseless females who willingly submitted to my bidding. They began in the third grade. As a ten-year-old, I had tried to coerce an unsuspecting teacher into the bathroom. My young intentions had been foiled, and no one found out what was going on in my mind.

Now as a teenager I was able to carry on a fairly normal life. Girlfriends came and went, and no one suspected the darkness that plagued my thinking. Alcohol and drugs became a part of the routine, partly to enter into the realm of fun and pleasure, but mostly to numb the deep pain I felt inside. The hard-core pornography that I had been introduced to as a young boy continued to be at my fingertips but failed to fully satisfy the driving urges within. Since I played the guitar in a local band, I found myself in a world of partying and clubs. Here there were plenty of sexual escapades to be found, but they, too, left me wanting. More and more the desire welled within me to do something deviant. Easy sex left me empty. I wanted to take someone illicitly to satiate the drive inside. Within a matter of time, I had become fully addicted to lust, and a sense of hopelessness and despair overwhelmed my life. There was an escape, however. The escape was my fantasy world.

At twenty-three I was now a man and had hit a place of sheer desperation. My girlfriend had broken up with me, I had lost my job, and I was hopelessly entangled in the world of alcohol and drugs. The fantasies, which were once a place of retreat, were now controlling me as I wrestled with ever increasing images of sexual conquest and obsessive control. What I once entertained as a sensual pleasure had now become a dreaded beast of oppression in my own mind. The beast was taking over, and I seemed unable to fend it off. I had no ability to close off the images, and I found myself being dragged under their influence. Plagued by the fantasies and fearful of coming to the point of acting them out, I sought help from a counselor and found myself in a treatment center for a month. I also joined a local recovery group and was immediately surrounded by support and encouragement as I wrestled with the addiction to alcohol.

This group proved to be a great place to deal with my alcohol problem. I was successful in breaking free from its numbing effects and was soon engaged in the program. I began pouring my life into helping others under the hold of the addiction. But there was still something I could never reveal, even to my closest companions. It was what lay at the core of my being. It's what was driving the alcohol addiction. The alcohol had brought numbness to the pain and given me a way to cope with the dreaded beast within me. Even though I was free of the drugs and alcohol, this secret part of my life continued to bring torment and wreak havoc. There was no place to go, and I felt stuck trying to suppress the urges within without the medicating effects of alcohol.

However, at twenty-six, through a desperate surge of willpower and applying the principles I had learned, I was able to hold down a steady job. I married a beautiful lady, and we had three incredible children. On the surface life seemed normal, and I was able to carry on with work and family without anyone being aware of the small but lethal part of my heart that carried the dreaded fantasies. This would be my secret, and I would take it to my grave. So far I seemed to be able to manage it all and keep things in check.

Then crisis hit. I lost my job again and became desperate to find a way to support my family. The crisis grew in dimension. The fantasies escalated, and I found myself firmly under their control. I was desperate. I really didn't believe that God existed, yet I found myself crying out into the empty air, with something deep inside yearning to be heard: "Take these things from me! I am desperate for them to leave! Help me please!" But in response to my pleas and cries, the darkness seemed to grow and envelop every corner within me. Its hold on my life became a vise-grip of superhuman strength.

It was then that I found an outlet. I rationalized that this was a way to satisfy the drive without causing too much harm. I would steal away to a secluded room, close the door, and make random phone calls, threatening women with bodily harm if they refused to keep me on the line. The pornography that had become a regular part of my life developed into a useful tool. While it failed to produce the desired rush I longed for, it served another purpose. Just gazing at the images before me worked like a drug to stimulate my mind and arouse my energy. It was like a kick-start, propelling me in the direction my darkened heart wanted to go. Since it was easily accessible, it became a quick fix that soon took over my mind.

I was now thirty years old, with a wife and three children, but I was under the spell of an addiction I had been consumed with for many years. Each time I made the calls I got the expected adrenaline rush as I heard fear, panic, and unrest in the voices of the women I called. Each time I found the fantasies subsiding and the urges diminishing as I satisfied their driving force. However, the diminishing effect only lasted for a short time.

To make ends meet, I picked up small jobs and short-term work for a time, but life was becoming more unbearable and desperate. Maybe I could make some much-needed income in Central City or Black Hawk, two Colorado towns open for gambling. I took six hundred dollars with me and drove to the casino. As luck would have it, when the day ended I had lost it all. Driving home I felt confused, scared, and depressed. The lure of my fantasy world stood before me and provided me an easy place to escape from .the crushing internal pain. As I entertained the dark world of my illusions, I remembered a cabin that belonged to a friend of the family. I had been given an open invitation to use it any time, and now seemed like the perfect time. I could stop by the cabin, make some phone calls anonymously, and no one would be the wiser. It was 1993 and caller ID was not yet in effect, so I didn't worry about being discovered.

I quickly found the phone and phone book after I entered the cabin and began to randomly dial numbers. It didn't take long before the addictive adrenaline rush of threatening and creating fear began to consume me, and I found myself craving more. With my mind in this place, I was completely unaware of two young females who had come up to use the cabin as guests of the owner. When they arrived, they noticed an unexpected vehicle in the driveway and contacted the police. Oblivious to the events that were developing, I continued my intimidating phone calls. Mid-call a sheriff knocked at the door. I immediately hung up the phone and moved nonchalantly to open the door and inquire as to the nature of the visit. Just as I was explaining to the sturdy law enforcement officer that I was a friend of the cabin owner, the phone rang. The sheriff went to answer it. An irate husband was on the other end of the line. The officer put two and two together and the entire charade imploded.

After the arrest that followed, I was given ten days in jail and two years of probation with court-ordered therapy, a support group, and regular monitoring. But these things, as valuable as they were, did not break into the deep darkness of my heart. I tried to discipline my life, thinking that would set me free. While I had a fleeting moment of success, it wasn't long before the addiction returned in full force, stronger than before. Without hope that I would ever be free from these driving compulsions, life took on a new dimension of despair. I had played with the fire for so long that it now felt like an inferno that was ready to consume anything in its path, and I was without the defense to fight against it.

I could only share a small piece of what was going on inside of me with my wife. What would she think? She would surely leave if she knew what I struggled with, but then where would I be? There was no choice but to move forward, try to keep the misery in check, and try to keep life manageable. But it was becoming increasingly unmanageable. I wanted out. I wanted it all to end. The inner turmoil was more than I could bear. The addiction was driving me, and I feared where it would take me next. Depression set in. I was guilt ridden, filled with shame, and pathetic.

In this place of torment I formulated a plan. It wasn't but a year earlier that I had gone door to door in an upscale neighborhood looking for work. As a cabinetmaker and wood finisher, I was sure to find someone with a household job who would hire me. Secretly I also hoped that there would be some female home alone during one of my workdays. I entertained the notion that this just might give me an opportunity to satisfy the drive of my sexual addictions or make a little much-needed income.

I remembered one home I had been invited into a year before. The husband and wife had both been home, and I had measured their garage for a job. The woman fit the visual picture of my hoped-for victim, and my heart began to race with images of fulfilling my fantasies. I had noticed the row of Bibles on one of their shelves. Above the Bibles was a stack of tapes that appeared to be Christian music. I quickly saw an opportunity. With the intent to entice the wife, whose name was Rose, I acted interested in the tapes and asked about them. To boost my pretense I even stated that I was trying to turn my life around. I was hoping this would cause her to be more comfortable with me so that I could gain her confidence, get her guard down, and draw closer to her. It worked. She was oblivious to my ruse. She seemed quite interested and gave me some of the Christian music tapes stating, "Don't worry about returning these. Maybe they will encourage you. I know where to get more." I had accepted them but never really intended to listen to them.

Nine months later, I had remembered the home, thinking I might find her there alone. Pretending to return the tapes would make a good entrance into the home. Much to my disappointment an older woman answered the door and said she was a grandmother watching the children while the parents were away. I handed her the tapes, stating that I had borrowed them, and left the premises.

Three months later I came up with a plan. I would go back to the same house, and I would play out my fantasies. Maybe this would put an end to them once and for all. Maybe then it would all be over. Driven by a compulsion I could not explain, I worked the plan, calling her husband's office anonymously to make sure that he was at work. That day he was. I drove to the house and rang the doorbell. No one was home. What to do? I was determined to go through with this act. I had given up all hope of stopping myself, succumbing to the drive within me. Yet at the same time I sensed another side warring at the core of my being. I was a desperate man crying out to be free. Something, however, was haunting me, as I felt overwhelmed with a sense of impending doom. Deep down I knew I would not be successful. The internal warfare raged between the incessant pull of the addiction and the pitiful cry for help. I just wanted this internal hell to end. I knew it would end, one way or the other, this day.

I drove around the neighborhood for several hours, sure that she would return. And then I saw her drive into her driveway and knew my chance had come. As she emerged from her car my adrenaline started to flow. I got out of my car and started heading toward her house. Suddenly she walked out of her garage and headed my direction. Why would she do that? Initially it took me off guard, but I found my composure and continued on. In moments she met me, head on, in the driveway. Knowing from before that she was a Christian, I quickly worked my plan to bring her guard down. I reminded her of the tapes she had previously loaned to me and asked for their titles. I was hoping her kindness would surely lead her to take me inside in order to offer me the help that I needed. It worked!

Much to my surprise she let me in through the front door. Inside I was surging with adrenaline. My fantasy was falling into place. As I passed through the front door, I turned and locked the deadbolt. Then I followed her inside as she led me to the stereo where she reached up to grab the first tape for me to see. This was my chance. This was the time to move. My insides were screaming with a new intensity, "I'm really going to do this!" I came up behind her and drew the knife from my pocket. I pressed it to her neck. Speaking into her ear, I uttered the words that I hoped would make her melt in fear and comply with anything I wanted: "Rose, don't move or scream or I'll cut your throat." I had gone over these words for weeks knowing that they would gain me initial control before giving my directive, "Now, I want you to go upstairs."

CHAPTER TWO

Unexpected Strength

Betrayed

My first thought was that maybe he was bluffing. Maybe the cold, metal object I felt was just an illusion, not the sharp blade of a knife. With strength coming from the sheer adrenaline of the moment, I grabbed his arm and pushed it away from my neck. As if sensing my thoughts and needing to make a statement, he moved the knife a few inches in front of my face. *Oh, yes, it's real! And it's sharp!* My own thoughts confirmed the horror before my eyes. "No! Don't do this!" I protested while attempting to shove his arm away. Returning the knife to my neck, he repeated his command and included an additional threat, "Rose, walk upstairs, or I'm going to have to hurt you." In that moment I knew I would rather die than go upstairs with this man, so I continued the struggle to push his arm away, saying, "No, don't do this!" Frustrated with my actions, he made another threat, "Rose, quit struggling. I'm going to have to hurt you." We wrestled briefly, and the next thing I knew, my back was to the stereo and his knife was facing my gut. With the little strength I had, I tried to hold his knife at bay, but I knew this would be a losing battle for me.

Spontaneously I opened my mouth and began to pray. To my amazement the voice that spoke out was not a weak, shaky one, but was strong, loud, and steady. I don't remember feeling fear but only overwhelming concern for this man who was doing something that was sure to destroy his life. In my mind *he* was the one that needed help, not me. He was the one in trouble, not me. The words that came out of my mouth that day are etched in my memory. I cried out to God, "Most Holy God, in the name of Jesus, I ask that you bind the power of Satan in this man and fill him with the Spirit of God. I ask that you send your holy angels to surround me and keep me safe. And Lord, let this man know that you love him and you don't want him to destroy his life by doing this thing."

I looked right at him, filled with passion for the destructive place he was in, and I uttered, "God loves you. He doesn't want you to destroy your life by doing this!" Looking down at the knife facing me, I didn't feel afraid or panicked. Instead I felt a strange sense of courage.

The moment those words left my mouth it seemed like time was frozen. What would happen next? What would his response be? He just stood still, holding the knife toward me yet unable to move or respond. He seemed to be deciding what to do. He looked at the knife, then at me . . . back to the knife and back to me. An eternity went by. Then I saw him drop his head and let out a sigh. Suddenly I remembered a girl I knew in high school who was in a situation like this; she ducked past her assailant and ran for the door. I knew what I needed to do and ducked passed his arm. My entire body cooperated with the flight as I scrambled for my front door.

He followed in frantic pursuit, attempting to hold me back. I felt a sting as his knife grazed the back of my arm. When I arrived a few feet from the door, I noticed that he had locked the deadbolt, most likely on his way into the house. "Oh no," I thought, but immediately I experienced a God-given strength to fight for freedom. In my mind I could see painters outside working at the house next door, and I knew if I could just get through the door I would be safe. With one hand I was able to unlock the deadbolt while the other hand fought with him and his knife. The words that rang through my mind over and over during this moment were, "Be strong! Be strong!" As I wrestled with my assailant at the door I also recall thinking, "I can't believe what this hand is doing." The door opened, and I was able to get my arm out of the opening when he closed the door on it. It didn't hurt, and I had the overwhelming relief that I was part of the way out of my house.

The door closed on my arm, but I was still facing my aggressor on the inside. He then began a new tactic. He threw his knife down on the stairs beside me and began coaxing me to just pull my arm out of the door, close the door, and talk to him. He promised not to hurt me. Encouraged by having one arm outside, I demanded, "No, if you want to talk to me, you need to talk to me outside." Again, he attempted to get me to pull my arm inside, close the door, and talk to him. Again, I adamantly refused.

The next thing I knew I was outside of my house, on my front porch, in the full sunlight of day. It never even occurred to me to run screaming or to call out to the painters next door. My only thought was that if I could just get to the curb on the street, which was in open daylight, I would be safe.

Probably in more shock than I realized at the time, I sat down on the curb and tried to collect my thoughts. Then the most unusual and strange thing occurred. He came and sat beside me. I looked over at him and said, "I don't remember your name, but I have to pray for you." He told me his name was Matt. "What's your last name?" And he told me. Strange as it seems to me now, I closed my eyes and poured out a heart of gratitude to God. "Most Holy God, thank you for saving my life. Thank you for being my knight in shining armor. Thank you for being the God that I can trust. And, Lord, I just ask that you be with this man and let him know he needs you in his life . . . that his life is hopeless without you." Following these words, I continued to pray for Matt. I was oblivious to his response until I opened my eyes and turned toward him. To my surprise he was crying and shaking his head while exclaiming, "I'm so sorry for what I did to you. Oh, look, your arm is bleeding." Not until then did I noticed the faint drip, drip, dripping of blood from the knife wound in my arm.

Turn of Events

I had just uttered words that were guaranteed to elicit fear. It was a sure thing. Then to add to the intimidation, I produced a brutal knife blade and pressed it against her bare neck. As I imagined this moment, I thought my victim would give up in terror. Yet what happened next took a new turn. The adrenaline and the frenzy of the moment made it somewhat of a blur, but I had not expected her to fight back. This was definitely not going according to my plan! I had imagined a weak and compliant female, but, having met her before, I feared somewhere deep inside that she wasn't. Yet the insane desperation to bring my fantasies to reality caused me to press on. I had to distance myself from any thought that she was a human with emotions and dreams. In order to carry out my plan, I made her into an object and dismissed any thought of how acting out my twisted desires might affect her. But she was not succumbing to fear as I had anticipated. I was going to have to use physical strength to overcome her. I forced her against the stereo cabinet holding the knife to her gut when she started to speak in a calm and determined manner. She was praying!

At that moment something changed that threw me off guard. It seemed like she was gaining strength, a strength I didn't understand. At the same time I felt the energy and adrenaline drain from my body and realized that I was unable to even move. I felt frozen in time and powerless to carry out my intentions. When I had planned this assault, I had a sense that it could go wrong, but now I realized my plan was unraveling before my eyes. She was speaking to me, but I couldn't comprehend what she was saying. Was she expressing fear as I had hoped? No, she seemed to be increasing in confidence, not shrinking in terror. She was talking to me about God. Why did she have to bring God into it? And why was she so calm? Where did this uncanny strength come from? And why couldn't I move?

The next thing I knew she was slipping out from under my arm and heading for the front door. I knew she would meet up with a deadbolted door, but I couldn't let her escape. If I didn't take care of her, she could turn me in and I would be arrested. I had planned this moment, it was the drug of my driving addiction, and I intended to follow through. It was time for a fight, but where did she come up with all this force? Try as I might I couldn't seem to hold her back, and she opened the deadbolt and started to go out the door. I had to get that door shut. She can't get out. My life as I knew it would be over if she escaped. Pushing the door closed, I was able to keep her inside with only one arm out the door.

Now it became clear I had to use cunning and persuasion, as sheer physical strength wasn't working. Maybe I could pretend to be concerned and get her to talk to me. I needed her to lower her guard again, so I appealed to her concern for me. Tossing my knife down behind her on the stairs, I coaxed her with these words, "Okay, I'm going to disarm myself. See? I'm throwing the knife away. Just pull your arm out of the door and close the door. I just want to talk to you." She didn't fall for my ploy but looked straight at me and said, "If you want to talk to me, you need to talk to me outside." I was getting desperate and pretended real sincerity. Again I pleaded with her to give me a chance to explain. She would have nothing of it, and the next thing I saw was the front door to her home blowing open as if by supernatural force.

I was in serious trouble. My only chance was to appeal to her sympathy in hopes that she wouldn't report the incident and I could walk free. Grabbing my knife from the stairs, I followed her outside and tried to detain her on the porch, "Okay. Stop here. Talk to me here." She repeated, "No, I'm not talking to you here! If you want to talk to me, you're going to have to talk to me over there." In a swirl of confusion and disbelief I watched as she walked to the street and sat down on the curb. Pure panic took over as I followed her and sat down next to her in full view of anyone who drove by in the neighborhood. I was determined to use all my skills of persuasion to talk her out of pursuing further action. She looked at me and asked my name. Butter her up, look repentant, ramp up the persuasion. It had always worked in my fantasies. After hearing my name she looked away, put her head in her hands, and no! she started to pray again. My fantasy was shattered. The beast within me had just been dealt another crippling blow. I knew it was over. I had failed in satisfying the driving force of my imagination, and I succumbed to the hopelessness and despair that now returned in full force. Now my only hope was that her kindness would let me off the hook.

Words on the Curb

The conversation that took place next was quite remarkable. I am astounded at how much of it is burned into memory today.

Wiping the small dribble of blood from my arm, I turned to him and said, "Do you know that it is nothing but the power of God that kept you from committing a horrible crime in my house?" With wet eyes Matt answered, "I'm so sorry, I can't believe what I almost did!" Over and over he repeated those words and then he began to tell me his own story of how he was currently under probation and in counseling for making threatening phone calls to females. He shared that he had been arrested a couple of years earlier and had tried to seek help, but instead of getting better the problem had only become worse. He said, "I'm desperate! I am 99 percent normal. I care about people. I do good things, but I have something that grabs hold of me and causes me to do things I hate." He said that he had this small part of him that was driven by fantasies, that these fantasies had become more and more out of control until he finally decided to act them out at my house. He then began telling me of his wife and three small children, ages five, four, and two and a half, who he loved dearly and who knew nothing of his internal beast.

So much to lose. If he only knew the power of God! I turned to him and said, "These fantasies are bigger than you are. You've got to talk to your counselor and your wife about what went on today." Then it seemed as if my mind saw the true reality and depth of his bondage. This was something that needed supernatural invention. "There is real good and there is real evil in this world, and you were under the control of evil in my house. There is one power in heaven and earth that can free you from what has a hold of you, and that is the power of God." I looked right at him and asked the haunting question, "Were you going to kill me?" With tears in his eyes and his head hung low he said, "I don't know what I was going to do."

At that moment a thought overtook me that I was quite unprepared for. I began to realize the horrible violence and evil I had just been spared, and yet there was another emotion that seemed to override the shock and fear. It was compassion for this hurting man who was obviously bound in the grip of addiction and pain. I saw him through different eyes than my human perception was capable of as I said, "If you had taken my life from me you would not have taken my eternal life because I know that I'm safe in the hands of God. But your life will be destroyed unless you find God in your life." Quietly yet distinctly he uttered, "I need a savior."

There was an answer for him. I looked right at him and said, "Jesus Christ is your Savior. You can find him in the Bible. You can start by reading the book of John. There you will discover your Savior." I knew there was hope for him no matter how dismal his story. I had found the power and peace of God in my own life and longed for him to find it too. He looked at me and said, "I'll do anything you say." While realizing that he was in a place of desperation after committing a crime, I was still struck with the uncanny nature of the situation. Here was a man who, just moments earlier, had expected me to say, "I'll do anything you say," and now, because of the intervention of God, he was saying those same words to me.

Still somewhat in a place of shock I said, "I don't know what I'm going to do about this, but I need your name and phone number so I can get in touch with you. I want you to go to your car and get a paper and pencil and write down your name for me." He glanced at his car parked up the street and said, "I don't think I have a pencil and paper in my car." Remembering the painters still working on the back of my neighbor's house, I replied, "Then let's go ask the painters." His response was as I expected, "I'll go check my car." Within a few moments he returned to me with a small piece of paper on which he had scribbled his phone number. Not only did he give me his phone number but he gave me the name of his wife and wrote down the names and ages of his three children. I still have the paper. Turning to him I said, "I forgive you, and I am committed to praying for you every day so that you will find release from what has a grip on you. I am also committed to seeing that you get the help you need so that you will never do this to another lady again in your life. God is fighting for you. He has already started working in your life. You came face to face with the power of God, and he has already kept you from committing a horrible crime."

I truly didn't know what to do next, but I just knew that I needed to get to my husband's office and talk to him. Still overwhelmed and numb with the events of the last hour, I tried to grab hold of my thoughts. Looking to Matt I said, "I'm going to sit here and watch you go." He stood up, walked to his car, and drove away with a tear-stained face.

CHAPTER THREE

Aftermath of Emotion

Broken

Walking to my car, I felt as though my insides were pouring out onto the street, as if I could see my mind, heart, and soul spilling out, reducing me to an empty shell. Sliding into the car, shaking from emotion, I gripped the key and turned on the ignition. My mind was still racing, trying to catch up with what had just happened. Adrenaline had been pumping through my veins all morning, and now the pounding of my heart caused my vision to blur. "What am I going to do?" I had neglected to make any plan after this moment. In fact, I had not even thought about my life after today.

My heart continued to pound in my chest as I tried to take stock of my situation . . . flat broke and pretty much out of gas. Where would I go? I briefly saw my life fading into dark oblivion and felt a strange relief at the thought. Wouldn't that just make everything easier? Wouldn't it spare my family the grief they were yet to face? Wouldn't it be better for everyone involved if I just disappeared into nothingness? A passing car broke through the sinking darkness of my thoughts and abruptly brought me back to the reality of my desperate situation. It was as if something deep inside me spoke; I couldn't ignore the words, "You cannot run from what you have just done." I started home, hoping the fuel in my tank would get me there.

Not sure of what to expect, I walked through the front door and was met by my questioning wife. "It is the middle of the day, and you are not at work? What's going on?" She was asking with a bewildering kindness in her voice, and I felt a crushing pain inside when I thought of what she didn't yet know. She looked so innocent and pretty with her long silken hair and gentle smile. Oh, how could I hurt her? I mumbled something, hoping she would give up her questions and return to her work, but she kept pressing. Finally I confided, "I have done something, but I can't talk to you about it yet." As I uttered the words, I looked past my now concerned wife and spotted my three young children playing in the distance. The reality came flooding in upon me like a churning tsunami. I had just destroyed their lives. I had devastated the world of those I loved and had destroyed the lives of another family as well. I had destroyed all of this when the only life I was really prepared to destroy was my own.

Stunned

Usually when I'm sitting on the curb in the middle of the day it means I need a brief rest or I am just enjoying the sunshine. But today was different. I sat in stunned silence watching Matt drive away and found my own head spinning with what to do next. What I wanted most was to be in my husband's arms. I wanted to drive to his office. However, getting the car keys out of the house was going to be another story. I couldn't imagine going into that house alone. Searching my mind for a solution, I remembered the painters working on the house next door. Without a second thought, I approached them and told them about the events of the last hour, unaware that the color had drained from my face. All three of them reacted with alarm and agreed to accompany me back into my home to retrieve those needed keys.

The three painters stood by, watching me collect my things. Inside I was shell-shocked and numb. It was hard to focus on what had just happened. Thoughts came floating through my brain, yet I found it difficult to retrieve them, like grasping for a feather in a windstorm. Suddenly one of the painters stopped short and pointed to the handle of the front door. "What happened here?" he exclaimed in confused alarm. As we all looked at the door handle, we caught our breath. On one side, the brass lever handle was pulled out of its screws by a good half inch, and on the other, the handle had dented in the great metal door by another half inch. A mighty force had torqued that handle and let me escape.

With thoughts swirling in my head, I opened the car door and collapsed on the seat inside. I somehow started the car and began the drive to my husband's office. What should I do, I wondered? If I report Matt to the police, he will be arrested, put in jail, and then just come out more intent to do me harm. He might be one of those repeat offenders, and his anger would surely make me his sought-after target. What could be done that would ensure he got the help that he needed? What could guarantee that he would not attack again? The realization that there was no such guarantee hit me in the pit of my stomach.

As I drove to my husband's office my mind was assailed with a barrage of conflicting thoughts that came pounding in like a cerebral meteor shower. Maybe this was all just a bad dream. I longed to wake up and find everything had returned to normal. But it was real. The person I had trusted was the one who intended to do me harm. Was I really that close to such a violent, destructive act? Had I just looked death in the face? At the same time that these thoughts were bombarding my mind, I also wondered how my husband would respond. Would he be driven to get revenge on the man who had just assaulted his wife? Would he act out his anger in an irrational manner? My mind filed through all these thoughts, but my body drove the car. In what seemed like a blink, I had arrived at my husband's office.

My husband listened in stunned silence as I unloaded the events of the morning. Every now and then he broke through with questions, as if trying to comprehend the disjointed ramblings of his dazed wife. I assured him that I was all right but then concluded with a plea that he help me pursue a support network so Matt could get the help he needed. My husband studied my face with an earnestness that surprised me, as if searching for the true meaning behind my words. After hearing me out he seemed to sense what was really needed and gathered me in his arms, offering his strength and comfort. He would honor my wishes. He would work with me to see that Matt got the needed help.

It was important to me to find something right away. We quickly located a support group for sexual addiction at a nearby church, and my husband called the leader to set up a meeting time. He then picked up the phone and dialed the number that Matt had written on the small paper I had in my hand.

It's for You

There was already something strange unfolding in my life. The phone just seemed to ring at the most inopportune times. Now just as I was trying to pry myself away from the probing questions of my wife, the phone was ringing. Well, maybe this was a good thing. Maybe one of her friends would divert her from my unusual behavior and my presence at home in the middle of the day. My heart skipped a beat as I heard her say, "It's for you, a Steve Pauly?" Was Rose's husband really on the phone? I had given my victim my phone number and now her husband was calling. Oh, was this strange. But what seemed even stranger to me at the time was that I was willingly taking the call.

I was quite aware that reaching for the phone could be dangerous. Most men would be coming after me with homicidal intent. But why would he call? It seemed crazy that Steve even thought I would answer, yet I felt compelled to pick up the phone. Much to my surprise, the voice on the other end was calm: What was the name of my therapist? Was I planning to talk to him about what had happened? After what seemed like a list of harmless questions, the steady yet stern voice on the line suggested a direction that seemed like a perfect plan to me. He asked me to attend a men's recovery program at a local church and gave me the name of the leader to contact. Oh, this was good. Maybe if I complied there would be a way to escape the wrath that was sure to descend on me.

By now I was eager to do whatever it took to minimize the consequences I knew were coming my way. Maybe if the contact at the church reported back favorably to Rose's husband I could keep my offense out of court. Yet at the same time I had readily revealed the phone number of my therapist. I knew this would result in the authorities being contacted, which would surely land me in jail. My contradictive behavior, however, wasn't baffling to me. In fact, I was oh too familiar with the battle that had raged inside me since I could remember; two forces, both warring within, working through me at alternating times to try to thwart the previous efforts of the other.

That night I went to meet the man whose name was written on the small paper in my pocket. A glimmer of hope ignited inside me that this sexual addictions group was my way out. After an initial introduction at the meeting, the man who was my contact never initiated any help for me or even called me back. The whole encounter left me frustrated and bitter. My anger flared at the apparent negligence of this man, because it was interfering with my chances of getting out of this mess.

Supernatural Consolation

That evening I felt numb as I sat on the couch watching my husband with our boys across the room. They were reading a story, and the usual game was being played as he scrambled the words and waited for their shrill cries of "No, Dad! It doesn't go like that!" It was a game they played often. Since they had heard the stories so many times, they picked up the slightest deviation. But tonight I couldn't engage in the merriment. My heart was empty, emotionless, just plain numb. As I stared into space, I drifted into an anesthetized land of gray, when suddenly the dullness was shattered by the sound of the phone. The voice on the other end was a good friend of mine. With halting words I relayed what had happened to me earlier that day. "Rose, I really don't know what to say about what you have been through today," my friend's voice was strong and steady as words of comfort and understanding poured out to me. Just the simple sound of a voice that cared revived my heart.

That night, as we got ready for bed, I found myself wondering if my life would now be plagued with nightmares. Would I have to relive this experience every night as a repeat encounter in my dreams? I was almost afraid to close my eyes and let myself drift into that place where my subconscious could take over and wreak havoc. As we sat at the edge of the bed my husband tried to find words to respond to my fears. Gathering me again in his arms, he spoke tenderly as I attempted to find the needed security in his embrace. My heart was beating wildly in the quiet room, and then he said, "Honey, let's just pray about this. Let's ask God to keep the nightmares away." As we prayed together that night a strange yet wonderful peace enveloped me. A tangible comfort flowed through me as we gave my fears and worries to God. When my head finally met the pillow that night, I drifted to sleep, assured of God's care.

Even though I had fallen asleep with a peace that I knew was an answer to prayer, I found myself wide-awake in the middle of the night. The room was dark and the usual creaks of an ever-settling house sounded louder than ever. I fought the urge to panic. Yet, almost immediately after I had awakened I started to hear a song in my head, as loud as if a stereo was playing in the room. The song flooded me with peace and a strange, yet real, consolation. Looking up to my dark ceiling, I thanked God for the comfort of this song and soon fell back to sleep. The next night I had a similar experience again and found that the song brought peace to my mind and a prompt return to sleep. After days of the same phenomenon I began to write down the songs that I had heard the night before, with titles such as "Great is Thy Faithfulness" and "Nothing but the Blood of Jesus."

The comfort of these songs became a part of my life for the next few months, and I never had a nightmare related to the traumatic event I had experienced. It was all quite mysterious to me. I shared this marvel with a good friend, and she looked at me and said, "Rose, that's in the Bible!" She showed me a Scripture from Job that said, "Where is God my Maker, who gives songs in the night . . . ?"[1] And later I discovered another in the Psalms, "By day the LORD directs his love, at night his song is with me—a prayer to the God of my life."[2] God was breaking into my world with a supernatural comfort that met my fears in the dark and spoke of his restoring and faithful love.

The night of the event we had prayed for wisdom for whether or not we should report this incident to the police. It seems strange today that we were even wrestling with that question. However, at the time, I thought of prison only as a place where the rough become rougher and a convicted criminal more hardened. Was there another solution that would give Matt a better opportunity for changing his life? As we thought about this question over and over, God had his own way of bringing us wisdom. It was uncanny how many friends called just to say, "We really think you need to report this to the authorities." Our question had been answered. We had been given wise counsel, and we knew what we had to do.

The next day my parents came into town and went with me to the police station. We made the full report, and the following day a female officer showed up at my door to confirm the story. She took photos of the small nick on the back of my arm and documented the door handle still loose from being wrenched from its screws. I distinctly remember the amazement I felt as she spoke these words while leaving: "I believe the power of God let you out of your house."

Three days after the event my husband said to me, "Honey, I need to do some errands. I'll be back home in a little while." He had stayed home with me since my traumatic encounter, and I hadn't yet faced the idea of being in the house by myself. "Wait a second," I responded, "You can't go to do errands! You can't leave me here by myself!" This wasn't the first time that fear threatened to obliterate rationality. I was content in the sheltering cocoon of my home with my husband's strong presence ever visible. Why should that have to change? Couldn't we just keep things nice and safe?

As is usually the case, my husband's logical wisdom prevailed. "I can't stay home with you for the rest of my life. I have to go. You'll be safe. I'll lock all the deadbolts, and you'll be fine." I'm not sure whether he was just trying to bring logic to the situation or was weaning me away from the façade of peace that I had created. Either way I didn't want to hear it, but I knew he was right. In resignation I answered, "You don't understand. I'd feel a lot better if you opened up all the doors and I knew I could get out!" With a knowing smile he walked out.

Just then I remembered the words of a counselor that had been relayed to me by my mother. The professional had worked with women who had experienced traumatic events, and in his counseling sessions had uncovered a hidden source of continued fear. He had said that for most of us our home is our safe place. The world is full of many things that cause us to fear, but when we retreat behind the doors of our home, we feel safe. However, when something traumatic happens *in* your home, often it will take away that feeling of a safe place and leave us feeling vulnerable. I had heard stories of women in counseling for years who were unable to escape the relentless pounding dread. Was this to be my fate?

With these thoughts still echoing in my mind I wandered into the living room and sat down at my piano. The song book lay open on the music rack, and feeling dead inside and without much thought to what I was doing I began tapping the keys in front of me, following the direction of the little black dots dancing before my eyes. A few bars into the song I began to awaken to the words that grew more and more alive as I played. Tears began to run down my face as I began to absorb the profoundness of their message.

You are my hiding place,
You always fill my heart

With songs of deliverance.
Whenever I am afraid
I will trust in You.
Let the weak say,
I am strong.
In the strength of the Lord,
I will trust in You.[3]

This song was exactly what I needed to hear. It was like God just took me in his arms and put my head on his shoulder and said, "Rose, my child, I am your safe place. It is not your home, it is me. And when you make me your safe place then no matter where you are you don't have to be afraid." Again I felt the overwhelming peace of God that day. God was expanding my understanding of who he is as he encouraged me to face a fear so that I might experience his consuming love.

Glimpse of the Battle

Five days after my encounter with Matt I again faced another first. I had been dreading this moment for days. I was coming home to an empty house. I knew that in a few moments I would have to drive into the garage, get out of my car, and step into my home when no one was there. Now I know that doesn't sound like too big of a deal. After all, don't people do that every day? But it had become a giant in my mind, a dreaded encounter with emptiness. I was not unlike the child who had suffered a deep abrasion and now the bandage had to come off. Would I be paralyzed by fear, anticipating all that could happen to me in this empty house? I uttered a brief prayer to God asking for his strength and peace.

Stepping into my home, I was pleasantly surprised by the deep sense of peace that I felt. I walked over to the stereo and punched the button, thinking some music would help fill the empty space. Standing in the very place where I had faced the knife of an assailant just five days earlier, I heard these words coming out of the radio: "I'm under the blood of the Lamb, I'm safe and secure from the enemy's plan, No weapon that's fashioned against me will stand, I'm under the blood of the Lamb."

I looked up at the ceiling of my house, and it was like a window opened up into the sky. I had just experienced God's amazing love and care in the words of a song, but I also knew that there was real evil out there. It was as if I could imagine a battle between good and evil. That day I realized that Matt was not the enemy. Matt was caught up in the battle, a much bigger battle that was raging all around.

I stood there living and breathing because of God's intervention a few days ago. I was flooded with the truth that there is a God who loves me so much that he gave his very life to save me, and because of his death I could have life. I was in the exact spot where someone had threatened to take my life just days earlier. I felt God's love as so real, so palpable, so overwhelming that it almost took my breath away.

At the same time the harsh realization came that there was nothing I could have done in my own power that could have saved my life. The best deadbolt wouldn't have helped me because I had willingly and unknowingly opened the door and invited my assailant in. The best alarm system in my house wouldn't have saved my life because it is set for the "expected" and this intrusion was clearly outside of the category of "normal." The best pepper spray on the end of my keychain would have been impotent to help me because I couldn't reach my purse or any handy weapon. Even if

I had acquired the skills of self-defense, valuable as they may be, I know they would not have saved my life against this surprise assault. There was no doubt in my mind that only one thing had saved me that day and that was the intervention of God.

That moment, standing in my living room in front of my stereo, is a moment that changed me and reset the entire trajectory of my life. That day I understood in a new way the overwhelming love of God for me in the death of Jesus, and his grace that brought me peace instead of fear, joy instead of pain, and life instead of death.

However, God wanted to drive the message home even more. The very next day I was sitting in my living room reading the Bible. I was still emotionally frayed by the events that had just happened. My whole being seemed to be shaken with the realization of God's love for me as I read passages of Scripture that spoke of Jesus, his death for me, and the new life he gave me. I felt like God was healing my soul after the traumatic encounter. He was sending his peace to replace my fear.

My heart began to ache for Matt and his family to know this love I'd recently embraced. They were outside of the comfort and peace that I had been experiencing, and something inside of me longed for them to find what I was discovering. On the curb I had told Matt that I was committed to praying for him every day so that he would never again offend another woman. Now, days later, my commitment strengthened. Only now, added to my prayer, was that he would find the love and healing of the Lord as I had.

Letter to Rose

The relentless battering of my mind continued as I felt the full effect of the battle for my thoughts. Whenever I had a good thought, it seemed to be immediately assaulted and taken down by the evil that fought to gain control in the very core of my being. I needed help. I'd always known that. I just never felt this terrified and desperate before. Maybe if I wrote a letter to Rose and her husband they would have sympathy for me and refrain from reporting to the police. The thought brought me hope, and I grabbed a paper and pen and began to pour out my thoughts. Right then it seemed my only chance for survival.

It was two days after the assault, and there still was no sign of the law. Maybe they had chosen to just let the matter die. I was desperate as I wrote.

> Dear Steve and Rose,
>
> I hope that my writing you this letter, or rather your reading it, isn't painful. I don't know how to say exactly a couple of things that I want to say, but I will try, and I sincerely appreciate your listening to them in this letter if you can.
>
> First, I thank you, and God, from the bottom of my heart, for your attitude and position in this concern. I feel your unwarranted love and care, and it overwhelms me. You are truly people of the Lord, and I cannot express my appreciation for that.
>
> It is so insufficient to say how sorry I am for doing what I did to you. My desire and willingness to make amends is great, but I know that some wrongs can never be fully righted and that my indebtedness to you will be for the rest of my life. I know that God will show me how. I believe that for now, the best thing that I can do for me, you, my family, and everyone else is to find a solution that will ensure that I never offend anyone again.

I'm going to church on Sunday for the first time in 20 years. I am and have been willing to do whatever to rid myself of this malady. But I can't do it alone. The avenues I've pursued so far haven't removed it. I want you to know that I am committed to finding the help I need if I have to travel cross-country to get it. I don't know who God has out there for me, but if my thinking is right, it is someone or some people who have experienced where I've been, I mean exactly where I've been, who have come through it with God's help and want to help others to be set free.

If Jesus Christ can save me, then here I am. Please hear me in this. You have my most sincere word that I will not bring any more pain or hurt to you ever again. I am sorry from the bottom of my heart for what I have done to you. I beg for your forgiveness and understand if you can't give it. I pray that God forgives me. If there is anything in my power that I can possibly do for you, let me know. I'll do it if I can.

Sincerely with appreciation,
Matt

It felt good to write the letter. It brought a sense that I was doing something that might better my chances. But that foreboding feeling just wouldn't go away. Not only was I looking over my shoulder at every moment, expecting the worst, but also I wondered if there really was something out there that would be enough to set me free. Were these promises to Rose just coming from wishful thinking and a desire to avoid the consequences of my action? Was I really still out of control? The thought haunted me.

Well, I better get started on my promised commitment, I thought. Where should I turn? I contacted a member of a twelve-step group who referred me to yet another member who was willing to meet. Sitting in a local restaurant, I shared my predicament and then waited for a response from the man on the other side of the coffee-stained table. This seemed so futile. What was I doing here? He wasn't able to give me the answer I wanted or needed.

A deep voice interrupted the conflict going on in my head. "Matt?" I quickly looked over, expecting to see a friend or colleague coming into the restaurant. Instead it was a high school classmate that I hadn't seen for years. Now this was a pleasant turn of events. "Well, hey, Tray, how's it goin'?" I asked, finding it odd that my friend was approaching me with such determination. "Not too good, Matt," Tray replied with a visibly pained look on his face. My heart sank. "Why's that?" I asked. "Well, Matt, I'm still a detective you know . . . I'm afraid I'm going to have to ask you to come with me."

CHAPTER FOUR

Navigating the Fallout

Booked

The anticipation of catching up with my high school friend, Tray, quickly dissipated. I felt as if all eyes were on me as I was led out of the restaurant and into the lobby. Tray began, "A woman reported that you tried to assault her. Do you know what this is about?" I felt the shame begin to mound up inside as if it would fill my entire being and collapse my airway. I knew it was no use to run from what I had done. With a voice that felt forced and surreal I answered, "Yes." Tray led me outside where I saw three police officers who had come along on the arrest for added support. Everything seemed to be swirling, and my thoughts were racing through my head: Where was all this leading? What was going to become of me and my family?

Looking squarely at me, Tray asked the penetrating question, "Matt, where's the knife? Do you have the knife?" Knowing honesty was my only option at this point, I answered, "Yes, I do. It's in my car at my house." I had driven my 1972 Datsun on the day of the crime, and it was still sitting at home out of gas. The officers followed me home so that I could give them the weapon. I knew it was the evidence they needed to complete the arrest, yet I was willing to turn it over. I knew it would be hard, but I wasn't prepared for the emotion I felt when I saw the face of my bewildered wife.

My wife had known something was up when she had received a call earlier in the evening asking for my whereabouts. Now there were police officers in her front yard. It was late at night by now, and the children had been put to bed. In the dark, I walked to the car, opened the front door, and lifted the knife hidden in the glove compartment. While the officers handcuffed me, I had the gut-wrenching thought that I would never see my family again. I asked, "Could I at least say good-bye to my wife?" As I was granted the request, I looked up to see her coming toward me, her face registering intense concern and confusion. Studying her face more closely, I marveled that there were no signs of anger in her delicate features. She didn't speak a word, but I saw love in her eyes. How did I ever end up with such a tender and beautiful wife?

As she wrapped her arms around my neck to say good-bye, my eyes caught a glimpse of three sleepy and staggering little children coming up behind her. My kids had somehow awakened and came wandering out of the house. Their faces were puzzled and their eyes big and somewhat dazed as they stared at their father, wondering what all the commotion was about. With hands cuffed together, I managed to hug each one hoping they wouldn't notice the fear and hopelessness in my face. The air was cold and chilly and seemed to hang around my neck like a yoke of lead. But it was no match for the chill I felt on the inside. I had ruined the lives of everyone I loved and cared for. I couldn't feel more worthless. As I stepped into the police car that night, I felt my life was over. I was entering another world, and my whole future looked as hollow and empty as my heart felt right now.

Tray was kind and accommodating as we drove away. It was obvious this was tearing him up as well. "Matt, I don't want to have to do this," was all he could utter at first. After a stop at the hospital for tissue and hair samples, we headed for the detention center. Tray and I were the only ones in the car now, and he had let me sit in the front seat for the ride. Time seemed to slow and the moments clinked by with a plodding emptiness, which gave me time to sort out the scrambled thoughts in my mind. I felt my heart coming to a place of resolve. "I am not going to run. I am going to face this," I determined. Looking over at Tray holding tightly to the wheel of the patrol car, I wondered what it would be like if I could just turn the clock back. Everything would be different and I would be free. We pulled into the sally port, the secured entryway of the jail, and I heard the large door slam shut behind us. It wasn't until we were securely inside that Tray turned to me and through a pained look on his face said, "Are you okay?" It was more than I could bear, and I broke down sobbing profusely in front of my long-ago friend. "I'm not ever going to see my wife and kids again!" was all I could utter. With an uncanny gentleness for the moment, Tray responded, "You're not going to be locked up forever, Matt. You will get out some day." At first the words stung so sharply that I found little comfort in them; then I realized I was desperately hanging on to them to provide a glimmer of hope.

Tray seemed to understand and nodded the OK when I asked if I could have a cigarette, letting me smoke in the front of his cruiser until it was finished. I knew this was not the usual procedure, and I took advantage of this small favor given by a friend. But the moment wouldn't wait, and abruptly I realized it was time to face the inevitable.

The booking into the county detention center took about an hour with finger printing, itemization of personal items, and a humiliating strip search. The orange jump suit was almost a welcome provision compared to the degrading experiences of the last hour, and after being given a towel, razor, and bar of soap I sluggishly followed the guard to my new home—a two-man cell. It was now almost midnight and my new roommate was already asleep. Climbing to the top bunk,

I laid down on the hard board that was to be my new bed and buried my face in the stiff plastic pillow. I felt like an empty shell of a man. Despair set in like a flood engulfing my entire being as I closed my eyes, not to pray, but to cry. The tears flowed until the exhausted ducts ran dry and a fitful sleep overcame me.

Letter to Matt

A week had passed since the event that had rocked my world. Deep down inside I knew that life would never be the same again. Some things happen in a moment of time and the reality of change comes seeping into the core of your being like ink on a cotton ball. But I felt confused. I should be consumed by fear and dread, my heart riddled by moroseness. After all, a lethal weapon had been moments from snuffing my life from me. Isn't that enough to drag one down into the depths of anxious and debilitating self-preservation? But the opposite was true. Instead of fear I was overwhelmed with an uncanny peace. In place of the dread, I felt an expectation for what yet lay ahead. Rather than an incapacitating anxiety, I felt an unexplainable serenity. Instead of shame, I felt love. Truly, I had never felt so loved in my life. It was as if I was a new bride and every cell in my body was alive with a sense of joy. This made little sense to me, and I started wondering if I was walking in some kind of unhealthy denial. Yet I was able to talk about my encounter with an assailant to trusted friends and find that my heart continued to reside in a place of peace.

It was then that I realized how many family members and friends were praying for me. Hearing about all those prayers gave me, once again, a sense of God's love and his presence in my life.

God had protected me from my assailant, and now he was surrounding me with peace in my life.

My thoughts turned to Matt. I had heard that he had been arrested, but I knew little more. I could only imagine the dark world of alienation he must be experiencing. Maybe a letter would reach him. I picked up a pen and began to write. I told him how he had been on my heart and that I had been praying for him and his family. The story of what had happened between us had gone out to my friends and to friends of friends. He had many people praying for him. I also told him that I knew God was fighting for him too. In my letter I wrote:

> *Matt, God is fighting for you. He allowed you to come into my home, and He allowed you to see with your own eyes the power of God . . . . He stayed your hand and kept you from committing a horrible crime. God loves you, Matt. He loves you so much that He sent His Son Jesus to our world to die for you so that you could be free from the power of your enemy. Jesus Christ came to rescue you. He is your Savior.*

I went on to tell him that ever since I had received his letter, I had been praying that God would send someone to encourage him and that God would help him in everything that would happen to him and with every person he would meet. I wanted him to have the peace of God I felt. I continued:

> *Matt, I know He will answer these prayers and I know He can use all that has happened for good. . . . But the choice is yours. Before you is the choice between life and*

death. Choose life, Matt. I am praying for you that you choose life.

I closed the letter by encouraging him to read the book of John in the Bible and by assuring him again that Steve and I would continue to pray for him and his family.

Sealing the letter I sent it off to Larimer County Detention Center with a faint hope that it would be delivered to Matt.

I Want Out!

It seemed like no time had passed when I opened my eyes to survey the dreary cell. Was this really happening, or had I just experienced a life-crushing nightmare and needed to shake myself free of its smothering effects? No, this was real. The memories of the last two days came flooding back into my consciousness. Months before the assault I had envisioned the possibility of prison if I acted out the fantasies that had consumed my mind, but this was bizarre. I now faced prison, and I hadn't even been able to follow through with my plan. Anger began to rush in, overtaking fear and panic like a torrent breaking through a dam. I couldn't even do that right! What had gone wrong?

Before I realized it, a defense mechanism began to kick in. I had invaded the home of a woman and brought trauma to her and her three children. I just couldn't let myself feel any emotion about that. Trying to stem the pain, I chose to shut off any thoughts of her. Right now I determined I just had to get out of here and fast. Whatever it would take, I would do it.

During the next few days, I was kept busy with more intake procedures until I was finally transferred to a permanent cell house. Now that the busyness of the last few days was over, it was just me and my thoughts. "What have I done?" The battle that raged within me for all these years was not over. In fact, it began to increase. The dreaded beast was still alive even though it had cleverly taken cover behind a new tyrant—fear. What would become of me? The stark reality of my situation became clearer. I could choose to be honest, apologize to all, work hard to get well, and accept any and all help that was offered, or just give up completely and descend into a place consumed with darkness, despair, destruction, and death. What I knew was there was no more energy to carry on a charade. My choice was surrender or death. That was pretty much it. Maybe it was merely for self-preservation, but that day I chose to face what I had done and to begin rebuilding my life from that moment on.

Then I thought of my wife and three children, and sadness, sorrow, regret, remorse, and shame filled me. I wanted out of this place. I just had to get home to them. See them. Touch them. Hold them. My heart felt like it would explode with emotion. My bail had been set at fifty thousand dollars, so I knew what I had to do. I wrote a lengthy letter to my parents, appealing to their hearts to come rescue their son. There was no response. With incredible audacity and desperation, I began writing everyone I knew using the only tool I had at my disposal: the pen. Yet in spite of my appeals there was no response. I remained confined and a world away from the ones I loved.

A clanging at my door woke me suddenly one morning. A guard informed me that I was to attend "video court." He placed handcuffs on each wrist and led me down a long hall. I had no idea where we were going or what this meant, but I dutifully followed. We entered a room with about ten other inmates and a couple of guards silently staring at a TV at the front of the room. I soon realized this was a formal reading of my charges by the judge who was speaking to us all from the screen. One by one the men were called and their charges read. I listened to each one and noted that all of the other men were here for petty offenses—things like disorderly conduct or possession of marijuana. Horror began to set in as I realized my offenses were far from petty and that everyone in the room would hear them and know what I had done. When my name was called, the judge spoke in a chilling tone. "You've been charged with first degree burglary, third degree assault, attempted kidnapping, and attempted first degree sexual assault."

The glares of the other men in the room felt palpable. I knew that even inmates with a violent criminal history looked at these kinds of charges with disdain. I felt fear take hold of me like the tentacles of an octopus wrapping around me and rendering me almost incapacitated. I would have to watch my back. Constantly.

The day finally came when my wife and children were allowed to visit me. This was a dream come true. As I rounded the corner of the cement corridor, I looked ahead and saw my wife's beautiful blonde hair behind the thick glass barrier. Three other inmates who appeared to be bodybuilder types in their early twenties were also there to receive visits. After giving my wife a "once over," they began to make catcalls and derogatory comments about her, using crude language to mock her attractiveness. Everything in me flared up, and I had to fight the urge to grab them and slam them against the hard concrete wall. The only thing that held me back was the knowledge that I wouldn't be too great at making conversation with my family after a hefty fight. It then occurred to me that this is how it feels to have the woman you love insulted or accosted by another man. Overwhelming regret again set in. If only I could rewind my life and have a do-over. Right now I would give anything for that option.

To this day I still have the faces of my children behind that thick glass barricade engraved in my memory. I didn't appreciate what I had until it was gone. I had been struggling with intense feelings, and now they were exploding with a pain that seemed almost unbearable. My two-year-old daughter sat on her mother's lap with a bewildered look on her face while my two sons stared with a mix of sadness and anger. It took everything I had to look at them and not burst into tears. My wife's face spoke volumes. Woven into her delicate features were love, worry, confusion, and pain. Neither of us knew what to do. There were no answers, and the future was a dreary blur of uncertainty. Yet that day I knew I had something to live for.

During my stay at the detention center I couldn't help but notice a large, six-foot-two, two-hundred-eighty-pound, burly inmate. He had a deep, gruff voice, shaggy goatee, imposing tattoos, and a known contempt for anyone charged with a sex offense. I had overheard him speaking openly about the penalty he would like to inflict on such an offender: castration and death by beating. Secretly I panicked whenever he entered the room and wondered what pulp he would make of me should he know my charges. Lucky for me he wasn't privy to that information. Yet.

All these things made me desperate to find a way to raise bail. Then one day I received an unexpected visit. A friend of mine came to see me and out of the blue stated that he was willing to put the title of his house up for bail. After sixty-two days I would be going home to my family. Even though I knew I would be incarcerated and separated from them sometime in the future, I wanted to tie up loose ends and have a time of closure with the ones I loved. The thought that I may not have this opportunity was more than I could bear. Now adrenaline rushed through my veins as I realized I was going home.

As I was reveling in this new turn of events, I looked up to see the big, burly inmate walk through the door to the minimum-security unit where I had been moved. He walked straight over to another inmate who had been present when my charges had been read and after talking for a moment, pointed at me. I could feel their eyes fixed on me and knew that my time had come. My nemesis had discovered my secret, and now I would have to fight for my life. Stepping inside my cell, I picked up the only weapon I had—my pen—and waited for him to enter. Every fiber in my body was trembling with fear. I was frantically searching for courage to confront this ominous being, the personification of my own internal dreaded beast. A large shadow appeared at the door, and I gripped my pen with a determination. Instead, my eyes fell on a uniformed guard who uttered three words I'll never forget: "You're outta here."

Confrontation with Fear

In November I received word that Matt would be posting bail and getting out of the detention center to return home. I began to wonder if the peace that I had been experiencing was from God or was just because I knew he was locked up and couldn't get to me. One evening a fax came through that said Matt had been released. He was out. No longer did I have metal bars and a well-armed guard standing between me and my assailant. He was roaming free. The thought hit me with new force as I absorbed this development. I had known where he was before, but now his whereabouts would be unknown. This was surely fertile ground for my mind to wreak havoc on me. Every noise and every creak of my house could become suspect. A fear that I hadn't known up to this point began to descend on me, squeezing in and pressing down with a suffocating force. It was like a surge of fear that had been held at bay was now breaking loose, and its overwhelming waves crashed against me, threatening to bury me in debilitating froth.

I gathered the notification fax in my hands and looked down at the ominous message. Suddenly I remembered a story in the Bible I had heard about a king, King Hezekiah, who received a threatening and intimidating letter from the king of Assyria who was intent on his demise. When Hezekiah received the letter, things didn't look too hopeful for him. The Assyrian king had come with a large army and had taunted the king and God, counting on the fact that King Hezekiah and the people of the city would succumb to fear and surrender out of pure hopelessness. Yet Hezekiah had an interesting response.

The story goes on to say that he went up to the temple of the Lord and spread out the letter before the Lord. Through this humble act, the king seemed to say, "God, I don't know what to do. This problem is way too big for me. I'm just going to lay it before you and trust that you'll know how to handle this." Well, God did know how to handle it. The entire army of the enemy was routed in an extraordinary way, and the ridiculing Assyrian monarch defeated.[4]

Taking my cue from a centuries-old story, I carried the fax into the living room and spread it out on the floor. It was late at night and my family had already gone to bed, but there in the shadows I looked up at the ceiling and told God that this was too big for me. I was terrified. As I desperately attempted to fend off the fear, I remembered a Scripture that said the Word of God is like a sword. It was as if God was speaking to me in that dusky room, "Remember your sword? Use your sword!"

I began speaking Scriptures out loud that I had learned as a child: "God is our refuge and strength, an ever-present help in trouble. Therefore *we will not fear*, though the earth give way and the mountains fall into the heart of the sea."[5] Then I spoke into the darkness again, my voice stronger, "The LORD is my light and my salvation—*whom shall I fear*? The LORD is the stronghold of my life—*of whom shall I be afraid*?"[6] As the words came out of my mouth, the reality of their truth began to penetrate my heart.

Something inside was changing. My mind and thoughts were coming into agreement with the words my mouth was saying. As I gazed up to the ceiling that night, I felt the fear melt away from me like butter. God used Scripture to comfort me and give me peace from fear. Sometimes it was a verse I had memorized as a child that would come to mind. Sometimes I found relief from my fear by sitting quietly and reading from the Psalms.

That night it was like the Lord said to me through his Word, "Rose, no matter what it looks like through your human perspective, can you know that I'm in control? If it looks like the very mountains are being swallowed up in the sea, can you still trust me to take care of you? No matter what happens, can you rest, knowing that I have you securely in my hands?"

It was a pivotal point in my life. I looked up and, with tears cascading down my cheeks, whispered toward the dark ceiling, "Yes, Lord, I can trust you." Matt had been released, and I had peace.

CHAPTER FIVE

Power of God in the Public Sector

Home Again

I just couldn't kiss them enough. Here they were before my eyes. My wife was looking at me with a comforting and gentle smile, and my children ran into my embrace. I was home. At this moment I had no thought of the future and no worry of the inevitable. I didn't even care if I died tomorrow. I had them in my arms and that is all that mattered.

For days I walked around in a euphoric state hardly wanting to talk. The smallest things caught my attention, like the metal fork I held in my hand. After months of disposable plastic tableware, this was a new luxury. Just to look out and see automobiles driving down the pitted asphalt streets brought joy and wonder. There is something incredible about freedom. However, I tried to keep my mind from wandering into the stark reality: this freedom was temporary.

My thoughts soon turned to my unfinished business. I had been in the middle of a large cherry kitchen job when I had been arrested. Would my customers let me continue and complete the job, or would they look for someone else now that I had been arrested? I needed to find out. I made a call and arranged to meet the couple at their home, hoping for the best. When the door opened a somber faced man looked me up and down and blurted out, "What happened, Matt? What did you do?" My heart sank. The public defender had cautioned me not to talk to anyone about the case. Somewhat sheepishly I responded, "I'm sorry, I can't talk about it." In a sarcastic and derogatory tone he responded, "What I read is you done near killed somebody."

The surreal world of my euphoria came crashing down like a bird shot out of the sky. Adrenaline began pumping through my veins again as fear and panic set in. Everybody knows. Everybody knows what I have done. How could I cope in this new reality? I knew what I had to do. I would completely block out every thought of my crime, making my heart numb and shoving aside any reflection on my eventual sentencing. It was just too scary and foreboding to think about. Self-preservation became my new task. Shutting out the future plucked me from the grip of a nervous breakdown, and I kept fear at bay by convincing myself that it didn't exist.

Over the next few months I poured everything into my work, focusing on the large cabinet job I had been allowed to keep. I also had to spend many hours in court evaluations, appointments with attorneys, and working on my plea bargain. The roller coaster of my life took me through the highs of family time and the lows of fear and dread that would break through the world of denial I tried to maintain. When my trusted mentor and friend saw my consternation, he offered his sage advice. "Oh, man, I'd run." Those words struck a chord within me. Yet even in my place of numbness I knew something about myself. I was not going to run. I determined to face head on what lay before me.

Time was racing ahead, and all my efforts to slow the process were futile, like trying to grab hold of the wind to keep it from blowing. One day, with two months to go until trial, my public defender looked at me and said, "Well, Matt, it's going to be really hard to keep you from going to prison." I felt like I had been sucker punched. The reality of my future again shattered through the fragile glass barrier of my ignorance. It hit hard. My shell-shocked mind tried to process the information. I'm really going to prison. I had settled on a plea bargain of guilt to aggravated first-degree burglary, which carried anywhere from four to twenty-four years. I had no idea what to expect. I could be going to prison for the rest of my life.

In March a hearing was scheduled, and much to my surprise, when I walked into the courtroom I looked up to see Rose and her husband Steve sitting with a crowd of people. My heart just about leapt out of my chest with shock and trepidation. Shame again flooded over me like a torrent. I couldn't even look up and kept my gaze on the floor. I could only imagine the loathing that they must have for me. Why would they feel any different? I had come close to destroying their lives. It was with great relief that the judge postponed the hearing for another month. At this point I just wanted out of the courtroom and back into the world of my own making, a world where I could escape the coming wrath that was soon to fall on me.

With renewed intensity, I focused on my family. I knew my time left with them was coming to a close. After that was a big black hole that had no ending. My future looked dark, uncertain, and hopeless. With ten days left before sentencing I sold most of what I had in my shop just to get enough cash to leave for my wife. As I methodically tied up loose ends, I decided a family splurge was in order. With some of the money I received from pawning my expensive hand tools, I booked a cabin in the mountains. For four days the five of us ate, played, and hiked, intentionally dismissing the haunting future that lay before us. But before we knew it the time had passed and reality returned, meeting us head on like a freight train emerging from the fog.

The saddest moment of my life was the morning of sentencing. We told the kids we were going to the courthouse and would be back, yet in my heart I knew I was saying good-bye. My three-year-old son looked up at me with a gathering concern on his face. "Dad, I'm thinkin' the judge is going to say you can come home." Oh, the innocence and tender constancy of my children. My father's heart was ready to rupture. And I had to turn away and walk out the door.

The Hearing

It had been six months since my confrontation with Matt. I had no idea where Matt was or what had happened to him since his release from the detention center, but each day I found myself praying for him and his family and seeking God's hand in his life. I knew my prayers were joined by hundreds of people all over the country who had heard the story and had committed to praying for him as well. Part of my ongoing prayer was that God would work out what was right in Matt's sentencing.

The court had told me that I could say whatever I wished during the hearing. I saw this as an opportunity to share in a county court of law what the Lord had done, and I began to pray for the words to speak. But no words came. Day after day I sat with a pencil in hand and a blank sheet of paper staring back at me. The day before the hearing I heard a song on the radio and the tears began to fall. These were the words I knew I wanted to speak. The pencil began to scrawl readily, and within a matter of minutes I had two pages of what I wanted to say.

The next day as I walked into the courtroom, I felt an uncanny sense of fear and dread hovering over the entire room. I found my body shaking and my knees knocking as I fought to catch my breath. One of the friends who had come to support me was trying to help me to breathe with deep breaths yet to no avail. Matt entered the courtroom, and there was unrest and confusion on his face. I didn't know what was wrong, but something strange was happening. Before I knew it Matt's attorneys stood up and stated they wanted a postponement. We were rescheduled for next month, and before I could catch up with all that was taking place, it was over and we were released to go home. What a letdown! I had been ready to face the challenge, yet now it would be another month of waiting. In the midst of this turn of events a new perspective began to take shape. "Lord, I know you have a plan, and I know there is a reason for the delay." Sure enough, there was a reason.

As we exited the courtroom that day, we were surrounded by our Christian friends who had come to pray for and support me. As they gathered to hug me and offer words of encouragement, I looked over and saw Matt and his wife in the corner of the hallway all alone. No friends were there to surround them, and I knew they had the weight of the world on their shoulders, because they didn't know what their future held. I felt my heart melt for them. I wanted them to know that our friends were not only praying for me but were praying for them too. The very next day I wrote a letter and sent it off. The words of the song that had brought me comfort and peace were words for them as well.

March 7, 1996

Dear Matt and Denise,

I know what we are going through is very hard, but I wanted to send some words of encouragement your way. All of the friends in the courtroom yesterday were there not only to support me, but to support you both, too. They care deeply about you and have been praying since last September for you and your children. We are all praying that God will give Judge Newton wisdom to make the right decision for your future. They represent only a fraction of the support you have.

It is hard to be in limbo, but I wanted to share with you some things that have comforted me. Isaiah 26:3 says, "Thou will keep him in perfect peace whose mind is stayed on Thee, because he trusts in Thee." Peace is a rare commodity these days, but it is a gift that God promises to give no matter what we are walking through.

I am sending you a tape that I have been listening to over and over these past few days. The song, "Love That Will Not Let Me Go," has really hit home for me, and I wanted to share it with you both. The chorus says:

There is a love that will not let me go,
I can face tomorrow
Because you hold me forever.
Stronger than the mighty winds that blow,
Safe within your arms,
Love that will not let me go.[7]

Steve and I have truly experienced the sustaining love of God and his love that will not let us go. We don't deserve it, but God gives it to us because of who he is. That is the incredible thing about grace.

Please know how much he loves you both and your family. I know your future is in his hands.

Sincerely,
Steve and Rose

One month later in April 1996 as we returned for Matt's sentencing hearing, there was a whole different atmosphere in the courtroom. This time I wasn't trembling. Matt got up and stood before the microphone and pleaded guilty to the charges. His attorney then spoke and, to my amazement, acknowledged that the power of God was responsible for my life being saved. The district attorney also weighed in and as a representative for the people of Colorado stated that it was nothing but God's power that had saved my life. Then it was my turn to speak. I opened the prepared statement, the one that had flowed from my pencil a month ago when I had expected the hearing to be held. With a strength and confidence that I knew came from God I began to read:

> *Last September when Matt entered my home, it was an experience that has changed my life and the lives of my family and friends. I know it was an experience that has changed Matt's life and the lives of his family too. That day out on the curb in front of our home I said to Matt, "Do you realize that it was nothing but the power of God that kept you from committing a horrible crime in my house just now?" He nodded. As I stand here today I know from the bottom of my heart that this is true. If it had not been for the intervening hand of God, I believe I would not be speaking before you today and I believe that Matt would be standing here facing a very different sentence.*
>
> *I have gone over the events of that day a multitude of times in my mind, and each time I am filled with an overwhelming sense of praise and gratitude to the Lord for what he has done. Matt said something to me on the curb that I have thought about a lot since then. He*

said, "I am really a pretty normal person. Ninety-nine percent of me is normal, I just have this little part of me that is abnormal, this little part that is driven to act out my fantasies." I am a nurse, and it is like hearing the woman with breast cancer who says, "I am 99 percent normal, I just have this little part that is abnormal." Unless that little abnormal part is excised by the skillful hand of a physician, it will destroy that woman's life. It is like the man with an occluded coronary artery who says, "I am 99 percent normal, I just have this little problem with 1 percent of me." Unless that man is placed under the care of a skillful heart specialist, that little problem will end his life, possibly in the next heartbeat.

Matt must come to the place where he is able to say, "I have a problem, and it is a problem that will destroy my life. I need help. I want help." If he can come to the place where he can say this and truly mean it, then there is help. There is a specialist for him. Matt came face to face with the power of God that not only saved me from harm but also changed the course of his life that day. It is this same power that can heal him and restore him. It is the only power that can heal him and restore him. And I believe that God allowed Matt into my home for a reason. God loves every one of the children he has created so much that he will go to the ends of the earth to let them know. I know that this may sound strange, but if Matt was intent on committing this crime I am glad he chose me. Not because there is anything great or mighty about me, but because I was able to connect with someone who is great and mighty. And that is the Lord.

Today in this courtroom Judge Newton will be making a decision for Matt's short-term future. Many people have been praying for Matt every day since this event occurred, and many people have been praying for this hearing, for the judge, for the attorneys, and for everyone involved with this case. We have been praying that the best decision will be made for Matt; a decision that will have the greatest chance for bringing about his restoration and healing. But there is another future at stake, and that is a long-term future. It is a decision about where eternity will be spent. And no court or jury or judge will make that decision for us. It is our very own. Every one of us can choose the Lord and choose life and peace or we can choose defeat and death. I am praying that Matt and everyone in this courtroom chooses life.

While I was praying for the right words to say at this hearing, a song began playing on the radio. The words said, "There is a love that will never let me go, so I can face tomorrow." I really needed those words then, and I need them every day. They are the words that I want to pass on to Matt and to his family. It is because of the incredible love of God that Matt was kept from pursuing a course to his destruction, and that same love is offered as a source for healing.

God is the only one who can perform the miracle of a changed heart. The prophet Jeremiah quotes the words of God spoken to every one of us, "I have loved you with an everlasting love; I have drawn you with loving kindness." Since this event, I have truly experienced the healing power of God. In place of the fear and anger and pain that would normally be present in my life and the

*life of my family, God has given an abundance of peace
and strength. And the peace he gives is real and lasting.
It is a peace and strength that is available to every person,
regardless of the circumstances that face them or the
experiences they walk through. All that is required is that
we come to him and ask for it.*

*There is a text in the Bible spoken by Joseph that
says, "You intended to harm me, but God intended it for
good to accomplish what is now being done, the saving
of many lives." I have truly seen that what was intended
as harm has been turned into so much good. Hundreds
of people have heard this story and have praised God for
his power the way he works for good in the lives of men.
Others have been able to accept his gift of healing and
peace just by hearing this story. For this I thank him.*

*I want Matt to know that he is loved by God and
forgiven by me. I will continue to pray for him and
his family.*

As I folded up my notes and turned to find my seat again, I
glanced at Matt. Written into the lines of his face was a sadness
and emptiness that pierced my heart. I could only imagine that he
was trying to absorb the bombardment of stimuli that would affect
his life for years to come. It must have seemed like a surreal blur
from his perspective. In the midst of my thoughts, I saw Matt's
slender and demure wife stand and walk to the microphone. With
a steady voice she spoke without hesitation, "I am standing by my
husband. I love him and am standing by him no matter what."
I was astonished at her words. The prayers we had uttered had
been for her peace and strength through this painful time. Her
commitment to stay was above and beyond what I had expected.

The judge then rose and read the decree, sentencing Matt to six years in prison. It was over for me, yet just beginning for him. Our entourage of friends stood and we all exited the courtroom. As I waited in the hall, surrounded with supportive loved ones, Matt's wife exited and headed in my direction. Without thinking through how strange it must have appeared to those looking on, we embraced each other, and I said, "I admire you so much for standing by your husband." She said, "Thank you so much for the words you said in the courtroom. I know God's in control." With that she turned and walked down the corridor.

Stunned by this encounter I turned to see my friend Bob standing next to me with a serious look on his face. "Rose, do you want to see Matt? He is still sitting in the courtroom." I nodded "yes" and followed him through the thick metal door. It had been six months since I had spoken to him, and it felt like a good time for some words of closure before he was taken away to spend time behind bars. What caught my eye when we entered the courtroom, however, took me by surprise. Matt was sitting in the corner of the room all alone. Everyone had left. The judge had exited, the attorneys had gone, the bailiff had departed, and even the court reporter was absent from her chair. He was just waiting for the guards to come.

Bob and I walked over to Matt, and his eyes filled with tears. "I am so glad you're okay. I never intended to hurt anyone." I knew he was saying through those words, "I could have taken your life. I'm glad things didn't work out that way." Matt looked up through sad and weary eyes and said, "Thank you for the letter that you sent. It was just yesterday that my wife and I came to a peace about me going to prison. We knew that no matter what happened in court today we were going to trust that it was in God's hands." Bob asked if we could pray for Matt, and he consented. It was a moment to appeal to the hand of God in the midst of a dark and confusing time. Matt was resigned to the consequences of his choice, yet he seemed to welcome this moment of prayer for his strength and safety.

When we finished praying, Matt extended his hand to shake Bob's hand, and then he tenuously extended his hand to me. I felt my own heart fill with an overflowing compassion for this man that only months earlier would have taken my life. I know it was not a love of my own making but the love of God placed in my heart. I wasn't seeing Matt through my perspective, but God was giving me his. At that moment I reached down and gave Matt a hug saying, "We really love you." He looked up at me with tears in his eyes that said, "I can't believe this is happening. I'm not used to this kind of love."

No sooner did the words leave my mouth than the courtroom again filled with personnel. Uniformed guards approached with a solemn gaze, handcuffed Matt, and filed him past us. He was heading to an unknown future of darkness and uncertainty, yet I felt like the delay in the courtroom that day was providential. It provided a time of closure for this chapter of the story. But I knew that there were still more chapters to be written.

Resigned to the Inevitable

The judge uttered those words that I had been waiting to hear for so many months. The sentence was given. Six years. My heart was flooded with emotion. Months earlier I had been told that my sentence could range anywhere from four to twenty-four years. The dread of being away from my family for twenty-four years and missing out on the entire childhood of my little ones was almost more than I could bear. Because of this, the six-year sentence came as somewhat of a relief. At the same time I was facing a future that looked like a scary black cavern haunted with the unknown. The hearing itself had been a blur for me. Words were said and testimonies given. At the same time my mind was so filled with the swirl of thoughts and emotions that accompanied this chaotic ride I was on, that I actually heard very little of it. I just wanted off the ride, but this was not one of my options.

Before I knew it the hearing was over and I was seated in a chair in the corner of the room. I knew that this was the place where the court guards would come to get me. It was the strangest thing to sit and watch everyone exit the courtroom. They were all ending their work session and would soon be heading for lunch, possibly ending just another routine morning in their busy week. Yet for me, this was the turning point of my entire life. I knew that I had no one to blame but myself, and there was plenty of that to dish up a heaping helping. I felt buried in shame as I sat in the chair watching "normal people" exit the room. Finally I looked up to see that everyone had left but a slim and unobtrusive court reporter. Looking at her I blurted out the words, "I think I'm supposed to go to prison now." She glanced up and with a startled voice responded, "Oh, yes. Let me see if I can find someone to help you with that!"

I watched her leave the room and realized that I was alone. It wasn't hard to notice the open window glaring at me just to my left. It would take but a moment to slide out that window and be off on a run to freedom. The countering thought hit hard in my mind, "But, Matt, where would you go?" As images of escape continued to tantalize my thinking, I looked up to see Rose walking my way, accompanied by a man I recognized. His name was Bob, and he had come to visit me once when I was in the detention center. I was struck by the look on their faces. Instead of animosity or revenge, I saw kindness and wondered what this could mean. Rose's face seemed to literally glow, and she smiled in a gentle way when she saw me. This is not what I expected to see. Confusion began to take shape in my mind. Soon they were sharing words of care with me and telling me that others were praying for me too. I didn't know what to do when they asked if they could pray for me so I said, "Sure, I guess so." Before I knew it they were praying for my time in prison! Could this be happening? Could my victim really care what happened to me when I left this room? That seemed more than I could comprehend.

What happened next still boggles my mind. Instinctively I lifted my hand to shake Bob's and noticed compassion in his face. When I turned to shake Rose's hand, she reached down and gave me a hug and said something about how they loved me. I just didn't know what to do with those words. How could someone I had intended to harm have love for me? I was so consumed with my own sense of shame and unworthiness that I didn't feel loved by anyone. But I saw it in their eyes and I heard it in their words. My mind was just trying to absorb it all.

As I sat bewildered by this unexpected show of attention, I looked up to see the court staff returning, and I knew my time had come. Two armed guards approached me and briefly described what they had come to do. I looked down at my handcuffed wrists and began to follow them out of the courtroom, knowing my life would never be the same again. In the back of my mind a thought continued to swirl around like a leaf in a windstorm. It was the thought that somewhere in this crazy planet there just might be true compassion. A strange kind of warmth began to encircle my cold insides as I walked into the open hallway and said good-bye to all that I knew and loved.

CHAPTER SIX

Release from Fear

Confronting Fear Head-on

It seemed that in some strange way fear had settled into my very cells. The peace I had been experiencing was suddenly being pushed aside by an insidious intruder. The hearing and Matt's incarceration were now behind me, yet my mind continued to process all that had taken place. Walking through a near-death experience had taken a toll on my emotions, which I was still trying to sort through. There were times that my husband would innocently place his hand on my shoulder from behind and I would instinctively jump. Participating in the process of Matt's hearings had renewed some deep-seated fear. The first time I came to the courthouse I was trembling uncontrollably and relied heavily on my friend to prop me up. Seeing my assailant again right in front of me had been a challenging experience for sure. The prayers of those around me got me through the ordeal only to have the whole hearing postponed for another month. It was as if I was constantly battling to keep my mind on something positive because fear seemed to be lurking at the door ready to bound in should I give it an inch. I had experienced debilitating fear before.

My mind went back to a moment a few months before the assault when my heart felt like it was going to collapse with fear.

We had allowed our two sons, then five and seven years of age, to travel alone on a flight to visit their grandmother in Texas for a week. We felt comfortable with the arrangement since we could walk them onto the plane, and we knew a flight attendant would escort them off of the plane and safely into the waiting arms of their grandmother on the other end. All had gone well. They had enjoyed a memorable vacation visiting the Alamo, learning Texas history, eating tasty treats, and pretty much being spoiled by their beloved grandma. Now it was time for them to return home.

We were to pick them up at the Colorado Springs airport at two in the afternoon. From all indications their plane had left on time, and the boys had boarded without difficulty. As we stood at the gate awaiting the arrival of the plane, we noticed a dense fog beginning to settle in over the airport. Soon it became difficult to see even the runway. We continued to wait, then we received news that the plane was circling overhead, unable to land with the poor visibility. The minutes dragged on. As the outside air became thicker and warmer, my own heart became icier and colder with a creeping fear. Were they going to be able to land?

At last we received word that the plane had given up landing in Colorado Springs and had headed to Denver. However, we were told not to travel there, as they would land the plane and let it sit out its wait on the tarmac. Then they would fly back to Colorado Springs when the fog lifted. We waited. We prayed. There was no way to reach anyone to confirm if they had landed or even where they were.

Finally, our hopes were revived. News came on the loudspeaker that the plane had in fact spent some downtime in Denver and was now returning to our waiting terminal. Sure enough, through a lifted mist, we saw the large aircraft approach the gate, turn, and come to a rest at the jetway. Yet when the door was opened and anxious families rushed to the gate, the plane was empty! We stood shocked! It was with great dismay we learned that all passengers had disembarked in Denver, and the plane had flown back to Colorado Springs with nothing but the crew.

The airline, in an attempt to remedy the situation, would be providing buses that would drive down to Colorado Springs so that passengers would eventually end up at their intended destination. The fear inside me mounted. Where were my two young sons? Were they in the safe care of a responsible flight attendant? This was surely not going according to our well-thought-out plan. We were told that we could expect the buses to arrive in another couple of hours. By now it was approaching five o'clock. Our boys should have been in our arms by two this afternoon!

Sure enough, within a couple of hours, buses began pouring into the Colorado Springs airport. Passengers were arriving on two different levels, so those of us who waited were running up and down stairs trying to be at the right location to meet the incoming vehicles. Bus after bus pulled into the airport loading area, and anxious passengers flooded out of the narrow doors into the embrace of waiting family and friends, who hugged and kissed them with sighs of relief.

Finally we received word that the bus carrying the accompanied minors was pulling in. Parents rushed from all directions to stand at the curb, anxiously waiting to grab hold of their precious little ones. The flight attendants handed child after child to relieved parents, yet when all had exited the bus, our two young sons were not among them. Frantically, my husband and I yelled out to anyone who would answer, "Are there no more unaccompanied children?" The response came back, "No, no more." The chaos of arriving passengers and anxious families was rampant. No one knew anything. No one had answers.

My heart lay in the pit of my stomach. My boys were lost. The airline couldn't tell us where they were, and we didn't know where to look. When we inquired at the desk, all we heard was, "Well, some more buses might come." All we had was God. We were praying our hearts out, but fear was strangling our thinking. We were frantic, but there was no place to run. I went into the restroom, sat down on the top of a seat, closed the door, and let my head just sink into my hands. "Lord, my heart is being consumed by fear just now. But I know that you are real. I know that you hear my cry. You can see my boys even though I cannot, and you know where they are. Oh, Father, please bring them back to us safely, I pray. Today, in the midst of my debilitating fear I am choosing to trust you with the thing most precious to me in the whole world—my children. I know you are faithful, God. I trust you, in Jesus name, amen."

When I exited the bathroom I knew that my heart was in a new place. Circumstances had not changed, but my heart had. Somehow God was doing a miracle as he quenched my fear. Hope pushed my fear to the periphery, and it was so tangible, so real, I could almost feel it in my hands. I had been consumed in fear, but now hope was taking over. Beginning to form within was a strength that I knew was not my own. Again, I was being held. I could almost feel the mighty arms around me and hear the tender whisper, "Your children are in my care. Trust me."

The buses continued to arrive, down to the last one. We watched all of its passengers empty out, and with a grind of the gears, the bus sauntered away. Our children had not arrived. Numbness threatened to take over. It was close to eight o'clock, six hours after the flight should have landed. Just as the last remnant of hope was evaporating, I spotted a lonely, solitary bus coming around the corner far in the distance. There was one more! My eyes never left that vehicle as it slowly made its way down the highway, approaching the handful of people still standing in front of the airport. When it pulled past us to stop, my eyes fell on the most welcome of sights that I could have imagined. Two little faces pressed against the pane of glass in that dust covered bus. They were the sweetest faces I had ever seen.

Fear. It is one of humanity's most noxious woes and plagues us wholesale. It comes upon you when you least expect it. Sometimes it is well justified. It was only natural that I should experience fear when I faced a lethal weapon. I knew I was facing death head-on. I should have been immobilized in sheer panic. Yet as I look at that moment, God intervened and did something that still amazes me to this day. He allowed me to press through the fear that should have paralyzed me, and he gave me the strength and clarity of mind to do what I needed to do in the moment. I know this is nothing but a miracle. I will be forever grateful. I also saw his intervening hand when I faced a parent's worst nightmare—the loss of, or harm to, a child. Again, God took hold of my shattered and panicked mother's heart and infused it with a good dose of his own, giving me the measure of strength, assurance, and hope that I needed to carry on without crumbling.

Insidious Fear

While I had experienced fear as a reaction to circumstances that would naturally produce fear, I began to realize there was another kind of fear that lurked in the background, waiting to take hold of my heart. This was a vague fear that hovered on the inside, not attached to any traumatic event or real threat. As the days moved forward after the hearing, I knew that Matt had gone to prison and much of the ordeal lay behind me. Yet there was another kind of fear taking hold. It was a subtle unsettledness in the core of my heart, a fear of the unknown, a worry about the future, a dread of another dramatic encounter, or a generalized haunting related to the uncertainty of life.

What was this vague fear? It was a hidden threat, a fear that lay embedded in my being without detection. But it was there nonetheless. Could I live in a place where my heart was tentative, cautious, and timid? It would even seem justified. Weren't there enough calamities around me to cause me to hunker down in self-protective mode? Hadn't I been accosted at knifepoint? Shouldn't I be concerned about what the future held? Would I be able to handle whatever may lie ahead?

Four months after the encounter with Matt, in December of 1995, my husband and I were involved in another life changing event. We gathered with a group of about seventy-five people in the home of a friend to talk about the possibilities of starting a new church in our area. Little did I know what God had in mind for me or how many times I would have to step through fear, trusting him.

Flooding into our midst were those who had been burned by life, bored by the mundane, or bypassed by all that seemed significant. In the spring of 1996, we located a pastor who was willing to lead our fledgling group, and we embarked upon the summer months with enthusiasm as we gathered each week in different mountain parks. Sometimes up to two hundred people would show up, eager to connect with others and hear the words of Scripture.

One year later, almost to the day of my encounter with Matt, on September 14, 1996, Grace Place Church was born. Almost five hundred people excitedly packed into a high school auditorium in northern Colorado and launched the beginning of a gathering that would touch many people with the message of grace. My husband and I were thrilled to be a part of the team, each with a small part to play. Steve coordinated the audio-visual team, and I played the keyboards for the worship band.

Six months later I was asked to speak for the congregation and tell the story of how God had saved my life. The opportunity was one I wanted to step into, but the insidious fear that was brooding under the surface emerged. Stand up in front of the congregation and share the story? What if I couldn't find the words? What if I used the wrong words?

The thought of misspeaking or stumbling over my words haunted me, and I began to tremble deep inside whenever I thought of it. Yet, I knew I needed to do this. It was a fear I needed to face head-on. So I prepared and prayed. And prayed some more. The morning I was to speak I woke up at the crack of dawn and went downstairs to collect my thoughts and frayed nerves. Again, in an uncanny way, God communicated through a song. As I listened to the words pouring from the speakers in my living room, I knew God was meeting my fear with truth. The words that jumped out at me were, "The power is still where it's always been."

This wasn't about me. The truth of his power confronted the fear that was trying to hold me back. My lack of eloquence and shaky knees would not prevent God from speaking his story. The power still resided with him. He was asking me, "Do you trust me?" Facing my fear, I uttered a soft "yes" into the still air of my living room.

The message went well, and my trust deepened another small measure that day. A year later the senior pastor approached me with a similar question. Would I again speak for the congregation, this time on prayer? Speak again? I knew how to share my story and had become comfortable with that. But that was about all. Speak on another subject? I didn't have speaking skills nor did I feel comfortable in front of a crowd. Fear came to life yet again and my insides churned. My heart froze and said "no" while my mouth moved with the words, "Yes, I'd be honored."

Elisabeth Elliot once said, "Courage is not the absence of fear but the willingness to do the thing we fear."[8] I knew I needed to step into the fear. For three days I worked on the message in our bedroom, an upstairs room with an abundance of sunlight pouring through the windows. God met me there. In the peace and quiet of that place, he taught me lessons about himself. The internal fight with fear remained, but fear was losing the battle to a deepening trust that seemed to grow stronger and stronger with each hurdle I faced. The day I stood to speak I felt held up by an unseen hand, and a peace captured my once trembling heart. God had been faithful again.

Two days after the message I received an e-mail that would forever change my life. Our senior pastor proposed a question. Would I be willing to consider joining the pastoral staff? It literally took my breath away. Could I handle such a role? Would I be able to meet the expectations? A flood of questions pounded my thinking, and the reality of my own inadequacy loomed before me like an impassible mountain. Surely there were others better equipped. I had not even been to seminary.

Then the familiar question came floating into my mind in the still, quiet manner in which I had become accustomed. It was as if God was asking, "Do you trust me?" Again the battle with fear took place, but I noticed that fear didn't seem as big as it used to be. The monster that had threatened to incapacitate and paralyze me at one time in my life seemed like a much smaller creature. I realized that stepping into a pastoral role would mean stepping into a journey of deepening trust each day. I knew I would never be adequate enough, strong enough, or capable enough to fill the role, but I could trust in God's adequacy, his strength, and his ability.

In September 1998, I stood in the midst of a group of pastors from my church during a commissioning service, and I was invited into pastoral ministry. It was almost exactly three years from the day of the assault. A new journey and a new calling had emerged from an ugly event. What could have been a day of devastation had produced a new season in my life. It brought renewed meaning to a Scripture from the book of Genesis, "You intended to harm me, but God intended it for good to accomplish what is now being done, the saving of many lives."[9] God took a dark and traumatic event and turned it completely around and was now using it for good. My heart could hardly comprehend the grandness of it all.

After fourteen years of nursing and a short stint in graduate school for an MBA, I had changed course and now stepped into the role as a staff pastor in our new congregation. And God was dealing with my fear. With each new thing I faced, I still felt a sense of trepidation and inadequacy; but somewhere deep inside I knew that if God wanted me to have this role, he would provide the strength, ability, and wisdom to carry it out. It was his business, after all.

A New Relationship

Gradually another equally powerful truth began taking shape in my life. It started to come into focus as I read the words of Jesus in the book of John, "Peace I leave with you; my peace I give you. I do not give to you as the world gives. Do not let your hearts be troubled and do not be afraid."[10] I realized that peace is a gift, and I can ask God to pour it out in my life. He also has an answer for my fear, "Do not let your hearts be troubled. You believe in God; believe also in me."[11] As I continued reading the words of Scripture, I saw that peace is in the context of a love relationship with God.

Something inside of me began to come alive to a new degree. I had read these words before. Many times, in fact. Yet the words were coming into clearer view. The more I opened my heart to the love of my heavenly Father, the more I felt fear subside. This was a profound key to my life. My experience harmonized with the truth of 1 John: "Perfect love drives out fear."[12]

I knew that God wasn't angry with me when I was afraid. He knows that fear is a natural response for all of us. Experiencing fear doesn't mean that I don't trust him. In this crazy world it is likely that confusion, worry, uncertainty, and anxiety rise up inside without warning. But God made provision for my fear. He doesn't just demand that I remove it on my own. He dispels it with his own love. He pushes it out the back door as I let him in the front. Dealing with fear is not a matter of willpower. It is a matter of surrender. Surrender to his love.

Fear wants to make us slaves. It wants us to be bound in its entanglements and taken under in its grip. Living in fear is living in bondage. It is standing behind bars and peering out through the openings of the harsh metal confines. It is prison. Yet God says I am not a slave but a child of his. A child that is loved, treasured, and embraced. A fuller realization of my own identity as God's child, his daughter, also confronted my fears. I knew if I was loved that much I could trust him with anything this life would throw my way. I am his child—with an inheritance. His inheritance includes great gifts to his children. And one of those gifts is his peace—peace in the middle of the storm, tranquility in the midst of chaos, and calm when all around me is raging.

Fear Dispelled

Another thing happened that surprised me. There was a compassion for Matt and his family that seemed to infuse its way into my inner being. I knew even then that this was a gift from God. Not only did this compassion drive me to pray for Matt and his wife on a regular basis, but it also brought to my own heart a kind of peace that was most comforting. The more God placed a love in my heart for Matt, the more my fear of him, or regarding him, was diminishing. Love and fear can't coexist.

As time went on, the songs that I had heard in the wee hours of the morning slowly disappeared, yet I continued to sleep soundly. A peace spread through me in spite of the stillness of the dark or the distresses of the day. God was teaching me to meet my fear head-on, and I was successfully confronting it on a daily basis.

While writing this chapter, and in midsentence about the subject of fear, my phone rang. It was my mother's number, and I answered with a cheery, "Hi, mom!" expecting the voice on the other end to be that of my upbeat mother. Instead it was my father. His voice sounded strained and absent of his normal vitality. "The ambulance is here picking up your mom. She collapsed on the bedroom floor just a few minutes ago." He was clearly shaken. He had little explanation of what had just happened. He was stunned and in mild shock himself. Was she awake, responding? Yes, for now. "I'm leaving right now, Dad. I'll meet you at the ER."

Driving the twenty-five-minute route to the hospital was a mental wrestling match. It felt like there were two factions within my mind fighting for dominance. One was the side of fear. My head was flooded with stories of friends who had lost their mothers recently and were grieving the loss, surrounded by those who cared. What would I find when I got to the ER? What condition would she be in? How would our family survive the loss?

Unexplainable but Real

Then another perspective began to invade my thinking. It was the other side of the match. I made two phone calls asking friends to pray for my mom. They both prayed with me on the phone, asking for God's hand of healing and that the powerful presence of God would keep my heart at peace in this difficult time. It was uncanny. There it was again. A peace and love came flowing over me, and the fear melted away. Somehow in the midst of the crisis I knew that I could trust God. I knew that he had my mom in his hands and he was working all things for good. No matter what happened, no matter what I faced, I knew I could face it with his strength, his provision, and his love.

My mom pulled through that day. But God had brought his message home again—his message to me about fear. His perfect love had driven it out. I know that whatever lies ahead, he goes before me. Whatever I face today, he is already there. He is teaching me to bring my fears to him and trust in his strength, even when facing death, which is the most common fear of us all.

It occurred to me that even in this most haunting of fears—the fear of death—God is at work. He is able to bring his perfect love and peace into these fears, and deal them a fatal blow. What quality does life have when I am living in a fear of death? When Jesus said that he came so that I would have abundant life in him, he was talking about overcoming all my fears, even the greatest fear. This is hard. Death is inevitable. Yet something was happening in me.

The weightiness that comes with fearing death was being lifted. This fear was no longer the controlling force of my life. Instead, a peace began to settle inside that I knew was real. It was hard to explain, and I knew it wasn't of my own making.

As I read through Scripture and focused on fear, new truths of God's Word came into view. It seemed significant that the command, "Do not be afraid," is spoken close to one hundred times in the Bible. Could it be that this is one of humanity's greatest challenges? Is it a primary reason we become worn out or live in a diminished place?

As pastoral counseling became a major part of my role, I spoke with scores of people and discovered that fear was often the underlying issue; fear of failure, fear of rejection, fear of powerlessness, fear of inadequacy, fear of intimacy, and fear of death. Often when anger outbursts are present, they are rooted in fear. It is no wonder that God made dealing with fear a priority. It controls, diminishes, constricts, disables, and inhibits us. He desires to set us free from its paralyzing effects.

Everywhere we look we see economic uncertainty, outbreaks of violence, upheavals in nature, and hazardous conditions. It isn't too hard to be immobilized or paralyzed by consuming anxiety. But is this the life you or I want? Will we allow the volatility around us, or our past experiences, to confine us to a state of self-protective bondage? We could spend much of our lives worrying about what may happen, but at what cost? Scripture says nothing changes by worrying.

Slowly I learned how to face fear, both the fear that accompanies life's challenges as well as the vague fear that wants to hold us captive. I learned that God is bigger than all my storms, just as he proved on the Sea of Galilee long ago with his disciples. They fell into full-blown fear when they tried to row their boat against a storm that was too big for them. The raging waters threatened to drown their hope, the gusting winds had blown their energy into oblivion, and the black clouds had obliterated their courage. But Jesus was there all the time. They called out in panic, "Lord, save us!" His words to them were filled with hope in the midst of their desperation. "You of little faith, why are you so afraid?" Then he spoke. The wind and waves subsided, and peace returned.[13] I knew when I faced storms in life, I would trust him to do the same for me.

As I learned to face fear, it became clear that I had a part to play. I could choose what I allowed my mind to focus upon. The more I dwelt on the problem, the challenge, or the thing feared, the bigger it seemed to become. If I let it, fear took root in the fertile ground of my own mind. But when I chose to focus attention on the capability of my faithful God, something began to change on the inside. The internal picture of overcoming the challenge or difficulty that I faced began to override the anxieties within.

I have a choice to make about where my thoughts are directed. Philippians tells me to focus on things true, noble, right, and admirable.[14] This wise counsel follows words that speak of the peace of God, which guards my heart, and phrases that encourage me not to be anxious.[15] Conquering anxiety and embracing peace is woven together with what I choose to think about.

This was a great discovery. In order to help direct my thoughts I began to journal, writing down what I wished to focus my attention upon. When I faced a large hurdle, I journaled about the strength and ability of God. When I looked fear in the face, I wrote about the courage that God gives and penned the words of Scripture that spoke of his power in the storms and struggles of life. When I found my own heart becoming faint, I concentrated on Jesus, who always shows himself faithful to those who trust in him.

I jotted down his capable attributes and willingness to come to my aid. There was a transformation of my thinking in the writing. While I could rehearse the difficulty with a friend, and sometimes did, I found the greatest strength and peace coming from this time of redirecting my attention. It continues to be a tangible way I overcome the tendency of my mind to become absorbed in the difficulty at hand. This isn't denial. I know the problem exists and looms before me. But now there is a new perspective and a renewed resolution to face it.

This made me realize that my "self-talk" mattered. I could choose to bring it into alignment with God's view of things, or I could let it swirl around in my own defeatism. Seeing things in God's way is seeing things through the lens of victory—victory over fear. Adjusting my self-talk is a process of learning. Without realizing it I can fall into old patterns and begin to find myself absorbed in the futility of worrying about the unknown. It is then that I remember a great truth again. There is a God who has my life story in his hands. He is able to bring me to his desired end—a place safe in his care and grace. He can be trusted. The disappointments, struggles, and hardships that I face on a daily basis do not define the journey. They are bumps in the road, but the road is going somewhere, and I am confident that God has my destination secured. My fears can be confronted. My fears can be fought. And my fears can be conquered. I do not have to live life in a subpar place of timidity, panic, anxiety, faint-heartedness, or diminished potential.

God was faithful and provided what I needed to fulfill my new role. As I walked through each new challenge, my husband continued to provide a place of support and understanding. Many times he would hold me in his arms, pray for me, and speak encouragement to me when I became overwhelmed. Often our thoughts would turn to Matt and his family, and we would offer a prayer on his behalf as well. We asked that God would meet his fears and bring him, too, peace in the middle of the storm.

I still remember the day when I took a deep breath and looked down at the closed gray casket looming before me. It was the first funeral that I was to perform as a pastor, and the elderly woman who had died was a friend. My eyes studied the faces of her grieving family, and my heart went out to them at their great loss. Would the words come? Would I be able to provide the message of comfort that they needed? A thought from Hebrews came to mind: "'Never will I leave you; never will I forsake you.' So we say with confidence, 'The Lord is my helper; I will not be afraid.'"[16] I clung to those words and stepped to the pulpit feeling, again, held in his mighty hand. I was learning to face the fear and find that God would come through. He just wanted me to step out and trust him.

CHAPTER SEVEN

Relentless Love

Darkness Behind Bars

The warmth I had temporarily felt in the courtroom soon evaporated as I was escorted back into the place of my first incarceration. I gazed again at the cold plaster walls of the detention center. After being out on a bail bond and home for four and a half months with my family, the temporary euphoria of freedom and time with my family had come to a close. Now I was entering again into the place of silent stares, uncertainty, emptiness, and unbearable loneliness. I felt my own heart begin to crush with the thought of what may lie ahead and immediately decided to shut it down, preferring numb apathy to the pain of reality.

The next two weeks dragged on as I waited in uncertainty about when I would be taken to my permanent location. I was now one of "those guys" who was going to prison, that scary place that seemed like an ominous pit of despair and violence to those of us at the detention center. Not everyone had to move on to this next step, but when it was known that a guy was entering the Department of Corrections (prison), he was at once an object of pity mixed with disdain. Now I was that guy. I preferred that if it was going to happen, it happen quickly.

One morning a clanging at the cell door woke me up. It was time to leave. An acquaintance I had made named Raymond was also herded out of the cell pod with me, and we were taken to a waiting van outside. The air was tense as we packed into the van alongside eight other inmates, all receiving very little information as to where we were going or what we could expect. Our assumption was that we were traveling south to Cañon City where our sentences would be served. No one spoke. There was little to say. Yet the silence was anything but welcomed. For me it became a breeding ground for fear as thoughts swirled in my head like vultures circling their prey. Something foreboding lay ahead. I just didn't know what. The loneliness began to bear down on me with an intensity I could hardly bear. I didn't even get to inform my wife that I was leaving for prison that day. How could my life have become such a failure?

All of a sudden the van took a turn to the west. I knew that Cañon City Prison was a long ways to the south, and this route was not taking us that direction. Where were they taking us? No inmate asked any questions, and no guard gave any explanation. Little did I know that I was heading for the darkest place of existence that I had ever experienced in my life.

We climbed the winding road into the Colorado mountains and soon came to the little town of Fairplay. Since I thought I was going to prison, and that was obviously not happening, I nervously waited to see where we would end up. Finally we pulled into a stark facility and found out we were at a mountain county detention center, a private holding facility for the Department of Corrections. As we were being shuffled out of the van and ordered to walk forward, I asked a nearby guard, "How long are we staying?" His answer was a terse, "Oh, sixty to ninety days or more." I didn't know at the time that the dark world I was about to enter would last even longer than that.

The battered steel door opened, we were shoved a pillow and blanket, and we were commanded to go inside. After my eyes adjusted to the light, I could see that there was a large bay area with cells surrounding the perimeter. Each cell was unlocked and held between two and six men. There was no cell assignment; everyone just had to fight for a place to stay. Walking through those doors was the beginning of hell on earth. It was soon apparent that this holding facility was run by the inmates, organized much like an inner city gang where fighting for your life was the rule of the land. It was every man for himself, and the strong would brutalize and torment the weak. Corruption was rampant. Contraband drugs were everywhere, and guards were nowhere. We learned that the guards were afraid to come in, fearing for their own safety. The most we saw of them was just for a few minutes each day as they quickly walked through the facility, always in pairs, and then left us all to our own devices. Sometimes I saw my fellow inmates quietly conversing with a guard as drugs were exchanged for deals in this prison-gone-bad environment. There was no safety for the inmates. I was stunned. Nothing had prepared me for this level of venality.

It didn't take long for me to realize that I had to take on the character of toughness and callousness just to survive. It was like I was becoming a different person. Inside I was overwhelmed with fear, but outside I had to be ruthless, harsh, and unshaken. In reality this tough world was one I was familiar with. As a teenager I had learned to defend myself as I gambled with drugs, took on fights, drove fast cars, and lived life on the rough edge. In a way I regressed back to that old place, that self-protective mode where I knew if I was goin' down, I'd take someone with me. But when you are in an environment like this you do things you would not normally do. I was a non-person in this place. Those at the facility didn't even know my name. The only way the guards knew we had not somehow figured out a way to bolt at night was by doing a headcount. At the time it never occurred to me that I had once dehumanized my victim in order to carry out an assault, and now I was being dehumanized here. This place was creating animals out of men.

There was, however, a bright spot in the middle of the violence, fear, and anarchy. It was Raymond. We had traveled in the van together to this place after knowing each other superficially at the detention center. Now our friendship became strong.

It was a mechanism of protection, a life and death arrangement, and an essential bond in this place of manipulative alliances and lurking evil. Raymond was big, muscular, and tough. His exterior broadcasted, "Don't mess with me!" but underneath his rough outer shell was a guy with a good heart. He was a good guy to have on your side. There was some consolation in knowing that he had my back and I had his. I know that I would not have survived if it hadn't been for Raymond.

One day, one of the inmates came up to Raymond and me with the news that a group of burly criminals were beating up a slightly built eighteen-year-old kid in the next room. We walked into the room and heard screaming. Directly in front of us we saw a frightened and battered young man being pummeled by his aggressors. Raymond immediately jumped to the kid's defense shouting, "No!" and the pounding ceased. This was followed by four of us jumping into the fray to try to squelch the outbreak. It was astonishing to me at the time that in this place of destruction and violence, there were those who were doing their best to defend the defenseless. I started to appreciate my friend Raymond all the more.

Conflict continued in this unsupervised arena, and each day it seemed we were more like caged animals than human beings. The fighting was incessant and regular. One day one of the inmates stabbed another in the eye with a plastic fork and then participated in a group beating of his victim in the community shower. I found myself fighting just to survive. There were times when I almost killed a man just to defend myself and keep my own life.

Another man I came to know was Jack. He was sixty-three, older than most, and seemed completely out of place in this crazy and surreal world. He reminded me of the biblical Moses with a long gray beard and gentle demeanor. Jack would walk around with a Bible tucked under his arm and try to bring encouragement to the other inmates. Most of them just laughed him off.

I took a liking to Jack and found his stories interesting, especially the story of what landed him in prison for six years. Seems he was growing medical marijuana in between fruit trees in his orchard. However, what made Jack stand out was the day his wife came to visit. She was a beautiful lady, about forty years old, and we all thought Jack was a pretty fortunate man. Not only was he a pillar of strength in the midst of a dark and violent world, but he had a great lady waiting for him after he did his time and got out of this place.

It came as quite a shock, therefore, when we heard the news that Jack's wife had run off with another man. Jack was devastated and went into a deep slump. His normal gentle demeanor turned rough and unpredictable. Since he was a large man, tall and lean, everyone stayed clear of his anger.

One day I sat in his chair while watching a boxing match on the community TV. Jack went livid. Even though we had previously been on good terms, he glared me down, piercing through me with his eyes, and motioned for me to come over to his cell. Not sure of what to expect I gave Raymond a "heads up" and walked over to Jack. Suddenly he slammed his cell door closed, with me inside, and aggressively shoved me up against the wall, spilling a barrage of obscenities. I knew that with the way I was backed up, the only option I had was to punch Jack in the chest, and I was a hair's breadth away from giving it everything I had. He was an old man. With one strong blow to the sternum I could kill him.

At the greatest moment of adrenaline and fear I saw a dark streak come flying into the room. It was Raymond. He grabbed Jack and pulled us apart, averting the inevitable should we be left to continue. I was shocked and pumped with adrenaline, but I had been spared from something terrible. Raymond had come to the rescue. It occurred to me that great evil flourishes in environments like this one.

It was two full months before we were allowed to go outside in this private holding facility. We found ourselves trying to make up games in our cell, just trying to maintain sanity. We didn't even look forward to mealtime because the food was so bad. Rumor had it that the large box of horsemeat we saw in the kitchen was the staple the cook drew from. I tried not to think about it. This was a prison sentence within a prison sentence.

One by one, every one of the inmates who had arrived at the temporary detention center at the same time as Raymond and me were taken away to the permanent facility. Our sixty to ninety days had turned into one hundred and thirty-three days—four and a half months. Then, at four one morning, a guard shook us awake and uttered the words we had been waiting to hear, "You guys are going to Cañon City." Never had two guys been more happy to go to prison!

Old Territorial

Before our final destination, where I knew I would be spending years of my life, another two stops awaited. As we piled out of the prison van to see DRDC (Denver Reception and Diagnostic Center), I was struck with how clean, new, and well orchestrated everything seemed. We had been brought here to have a battery of physical and psycho-logical tests run so we could be placed in "real" prison at one of the permanent facilities. I was relieved to see that they had actual guards on duty making sure that sanity existed. I was again strip-searched and then led to my own cell, which was locked down for twenty-three hours per day, letting me out only for meals and testing. The crazy thing is that I appreciated this solitary environment after my terrifying days at the county detention center.

For one month I stayed here awaiting my final destination. The lights were kept on around the clock so there was never a true night-time, yet I found myself consuming the lonely hours by drawing and writing letters. I could now buy cigarettes in the commissary, and with them and my drawing pad and paper I whittled the time away, producing page after page of intricate artwork. Sometimes I would stay up all night writing letters to my wife. This brought me a measure of relief as I wrote of my questions and pain and longed for just a moment to see her face. It seemed like so long since I had looked at her or held my children. She was now trying to survive like a single mom with dwindling finances and increasing stress. My heart ached for her. What had I done to her? What had I brought on my children? Sometimes the pain of my own life choices was more than I could bear. The question continued to haunt my thinking, "Would I, too, lose my wife and kids like other inmates I had known?" Yet, drawing and writing seemed to provide an outlet of comfort.

Soon the needed testing was completed, and we were told it was time to move. My hands were cuffed and legs shackled before I was escorted to the now familiar prison bus. Inside, guards locked our leg shackles to the molded fiberglass seats. Two rifle-bearing guards rode in the front and one in back, intently eyeing us through expressionless faces as we made the four-hour trip to Cañon City. It was clear that this was just a daily routine for them, transporting hundreds of prisoners to their destination, and then going home to have dinner with their wives. Their world seemed so detached from mine.

We were taken to "Old Territorial," or the Colorado Territorial Correctional Facility, in downtown Cañon City. It is the oldest state prison in Colorado, having been constructed in 1868. I couldn't help noticing the imposing thirty-foot stone walls surrounding the old facility. It looked like something out of the movies. When we entered, I was struck by the tall three stories and narrow, tall metal bars framing the many cells. It was so loud inside. You could hear everybody. This would be a holding site until I was sent to my final place of confinement.

One day a group of us inmates were told that some young teenagers from the Scared Straight program were coming to the prison. These were tough kids who had gotten into trouble with the law, usually through petty crimes. The hope was held that they would be deterred from more deviant behavior and subsequent prison sentences if they could just be scared enough by the prospects of what may lie ahead should they continue to offend. We were instructed to cat call, yell obscenities, and intimidate them in order to cooperate with the program. We did our best to sound ferocious. One inmate yelled, "Can't wait till you get here, little boy!" The fear on their faces gave me a small sense of satisfaction, yet underneath I knew it would take far more than this to dissuade these strong-willed teens. It would have taken a lot more than this for me too.

In many ways it seemed like prison was reinforcing the very deviant behavior that had gotten me here in the first place. I was still trying to sort it all out. At times I felt like I was caught in a crazy tornado that was taking me all kinds of places against my will, yet no place that made any sense. One of the most uncomfortable places was the community shower, a large area with thirty showerheads. Not only were we regularly strip-searched, but this was a place without modesty or privacy. It was one thing to have to shower regularly out in the open, but the worst part was the female guards who came to stare into the showers when we were there. Again I felt that same dehumanizing feeling, knowing I was nothing more than an object in the eyes of another. Even in this place, it did not occur to me that this was the very way I had been objectifying others.

It was here in Old Territorial that I finally shed my orange detention suit and received a new green prison suit with a black belt and boots. Everything, even my underwear, was labeled with my name and prison number. At last I was ready. Ready to move to my own cell in the nearby facility where I had been sentenced to serve my years.

Prison within a Prison

It was now October 1996 near Halloween. On a chilly morning I was transported to Cell House 5 Lower. I had been waiting to get here since the beginning of April. This was a part of a prison complex that housed five thousand men. That day I didn't realize it would be my home for the next three years. There was a small bed in the corner where I would be staying and another bed on the other side for my cellmate. Strangely I felt an eerie sense of ease knowing that I'd reached the final destination of my prison sentence.

However, my secret was now out. I had kept it under wraps that I had been classified as a sex offender, preferring to tell those who were questioning me that I was here for first-degree burglary. But Fremont, the facility I was now entering, was known as the place sex offenders went. I found myself withdrawing internally and shutting down inside. It didn't take long before waves of shame, remorse, and depression descended on me like a black fog that refused to lift. The pornographic images I had filled my mind with over the years began a moment-by-moment parade through my thoughts. Day after day, my mind was tormented by the thoughts that had landed me in this place. The beast that lurked inside me was alive and well, only here it wasn't being fed. I was in a prison within a prison, and no one but me knew it.

As the days went by, the black fog increased. There was clearly no sign or hope that I would somehow find a release from the strangling world of my mind. My aberrant thoughts persisted, controlling me and dominating my deliberations all the time. I wanted to give up. Questions pounded my mind. Who am I? What am I going to be? A rapist?

When I had arrived, I was under the delusion that I would just sit in my prison cell and draw for six years and the time would somehow fly by. But that simply wasn't going to happen. I was told I either had to go to school or go to work. The last thing I wanted was to be in a classroom, so I chose to step into the prison workforce. Even though I was a skilled carpenter, I was denied opportunity to work in the cabinet industry and instead found myself spraying powder coating on dumpsters for Waste Management. I liked working in the metal shop and found satisfaction in putting in a hard day's labor. It would be my work for the next three years.

Even though I continued to be relentlessly plagued by my addictive sexual fantasies, I also found myself consumed with wanting to see my wife and kids. It occurred to me that if I could just get on with my treatment and complete what was required of me, I could move on with my life and return to normalcy again. If I had my way I would just push that proverbial button, bypass all the unnecessary hoops they were making me jump through, and move on home. And, maybe if I worked hard at completing the treatment, my beast within would wither and die, and peace would again be restored. It became my new plan.

I was so anxious to start on a treatment that I immediately signed up on the waiting list for sex offender, phase one. But time continued to drag on, and no one called me to begin the program. I guessed the system was just too backed up. The days turned into weeks and weeks into months until a year had gone by. My world continued to crumble from within. When I think about it now, I was living in a prison long before I entered the facility. It was a prison of addiction. I couldn't escape it. I couldn't voluntarily remove myself from its powerful pull, its incessant desire, and the euphoric feel when it was satisfied. No drug compared. I had been sober in AA for ten years but still found myself trying to deal with my inner torments. I didn't have control over my life. Something else did.

Even though I was now surrounded by metal bars, not much had changed on the inside of me. I was still imprisoned and knew that at any moment I could again succumb to the beast. I had no mental defense if a temptation presented itself. This was a place of unbearable loneliness. Before this, my beast had taken me to a place where I had used force to try to satisfy my lusts. I had objectified a woman and dismissed the idea that she was even a human being in order to follow through on my driving compulsions. I had to. It was the only way I could reconcile in my own mind the actions that I carried out.

A new fear began to take hold in me. It was the fear that the darkness inside of me was being reinforced in this place. Without help and hope, what would keep the evil I struggled with from becoming cemented and permanent? I prayed to have it removed even though I wasn't exactly sure to whom I was praying. My ability to even function was being hindered. I wanted so badly to react sanely and normally. I didn't want to be enslaved. Yet the torment continued. Often when I saw a female guard I couldn't get her out of my mind for hours and hours. The question preoccupied me, "Am I going to assault more women when I leave here?"

Realistically I knew that I would get out someday. But would I be able to keep my wife until then? It felt like my family was slipping out of my hands. I had really left my wife holding the bag and rarely saw her these days. Driving five and a half hours to the prison then staying the night in a KOA campground with three small children was an almost overwhelming task, so her visits were few. It terrified me to think of what I might become without them. If I was released someday but didn't have my wife and kids, I just wouldn't care about anything. Maybe I would go out to again fulfill my fantasies and not even care if I hurt someone. These thoughts were so oppressive that I would cry for hours out of shame and self-pity. I was losing the only thing that I really cared about.

Turn of Events

One of the great loses that I felt in my final place of incarceration was the loss of my friend Raymond. We had parted ways at DRDC, and I was not sure where he ended up. He had been a bedrock and my source of sanity through the journey so far, and now we were separated. My heart grieved for the friendship that had been lifeblood for me.

It was not long, however, before I met another man who was to become instrumental in my life. His name was Tad. This fellow inmate, who was truly a tough guy but who treated others in a gentlemanly way and didn't use profanity, which was otherwise the norm in prison, immediately intrigued me. I myself was pretty good at talking like a sailor. Tad and I worked together in the metal shop beautifying dumpsters with powder coat, and then we would head to the prison gym together to work out. Soon he became a trusted friend and confidant.

Even though Tad had come to the prison because of his own moral failings, he had found something that seemed to give him strength and hope. He talked often about church and Jesus Christ as his Savior. The surprising thing for me was that it didn't scare me or turn me off. In the past when someone had spoken of Christianity, it just freaked me out. It brought back too many bad memories of my childhood. I knew that Rose was a Christian, and I had tried to appease her with some Christian lingo at the time of the assault. The truth was, I really knew very little about what it all meant, and my heart was far from entertaining any such notions for myself.

But Tad was different. Tad read the Bible and really seemed to lean on a power outside of him. That was surely a different reality for me. Since the beginning of this journey, I had learned self-preservation well. I had to depend on myself alone to survive. Yet I found myself respecting him greatly, even though I really didn't comprehend where he was coming from. I knew he was a legitimate friend whom I could trust.

Life behind bars continued, and a year later I began the treatment program that I had been waiting for. I tried to apply myself, thinking that this was my ticket home. But the haunting continued. Deep inside, I was the same me. When it came right down to it, I was still out of control on the inside. There was no security. No peace. No place of escape from what tormented me. Thank goodness for Tad. We continued our routine of work and lifting weights, and it provided a sense of stability that at times blanketed the gnawing fears within. But the blanket was temporary. Without notice it would lift, and I would again come face to face with the reality of the growing gangrene of my heart.

About two years into my imprisonment, I received startling news from Tad. He was moving to Cell House 9. This was a good thing for him, but a bad thing for me. Cell House 9 was a place where the "elite" prisoners went, those with stellar prison records. It was a place where you got a thicker mattress and a few more privileges for good behavior. Tad saw my disappointment at his news and said, "Matt, you oughta apply for Cell House 9!" My response was, "No way. I would never get accepted for that." But he persuaded me to turn in the application. To my surprise, it was granted.

Cell House 9 was definitely an upgrade, but my joy was short-lived as I received more startling news. This time it was from my wife. She called to inform me that she had become a born-again Christian.

This scared me. I knew about those fanatics who were all whacked out on God. Now they had gotten to my wife! My fear cascaded into pure panic as I became obsessed with a new thought. Now she would surely leave me for some guy in church. This might be a good thing for her, but it was a bad thing for me! Why wouldn't she leave me! Of course she would be more attracted to a nonviolent man.

At this time a new friend I had made in Cell House 9 stepped in to give his perspective and help me to see things differently. Vince was a Christ follower as well, and, as with Tad, I had come to respect him greatly even though I didn't agree with his beliefs. He said, "Matt, what if she does walk? Where does that leave you? What kind of man are you apart from your wife?" Okay. That really got me to thinking. Who am I?

I continued to ponder these questions for days and knew that something my friend had said was hitting me at the core of my being. Do I become a born-again Christian so I can keep my wife? Something inside told me this would never work. After some time, however, I ventured a question. "Vince, what does 'born-again' mean? I always thought that anyone who was born-again was kind of crazy." Vince and Tad stood together and smiled at me. "Matt, we're both born-again. You like us! We're not wacky." Then they looked me straight in the eye and said with the utmost of sincerity, "Matt, we can't describe the feeling when you know Jesus as your Savior and turn your life over to him. He will forgive you and reward you. He loves you, Matt." I immediately turned skeptical. I admired and respected these guys, but now they were telling me things that I just could not absorb or believe. Jesus loves me. That thought was too difficult to comprehend.

At the same time another thought came bounding into my thinking like an unexpected meteor out of space. I knew that I needed something different in my life whether my wife stuck with me or not. What was my option? I could choose hell. I knew what that was like. I had been living in it for thirty years. My thoughts hung suspended for what felt like an eternity.

At that moment I made up my mind. Something deep inside turned a corner. The tough façade of my own making had been broken through, shattered by some unseen force. My heart opened to a new place, and I knew I wanted to have God in my life. But what would that involve? Did I need to light some candles? Did I need to wear some special clothes? Tad and Vince were there to guide me in these questions as well. No, they said. I just needed to pray a prayer to God and he would hear me. They helped me see that he was already pursuing me and longing for me to turn to him. He was actually waiting for this moment! An uncanny peace took over the place of skepticism and apprehension as we spoke.

So there in the prison, the three of us, along with another Christian inmate named Jed, went into a parked semi-truck and gathered together. Four tough-guy convicts held hands in a circle as they led me in praying to the God I had never known before this moment. He was a God who had been there all along. I just didn't know it. Oh, I had prayed before. But in the past they were prayers of desperation to a god of my own understanding. He was a god who would do what I wanted him to do and act as I wished him to act. But here in the semi-truck I was praying to a God who was now revealing himself to me. He was showing me who he was, and I was choosing to submit to him. As I lowered my head to pray, flanked by the friends who had led me there, I felt my heart melt in awe and surrender. "God, I believe in you. I see you working in these men. I want to accept you. I want you to come into my life."

I have learned since then that not everyone has the same experience when they make a decision to believe in Jesus Christ. But for me, the moment of my prayer was a moment I will remember for the rest of my life. It was a powerful encounter with an unseen but very present God. My hair seemed to rise and my skin tingled. Everything in me seemed to have a supernatural infusion of new life and restored energy. It felt like a tsunami of peace and relief flowed over me and saturated me to the center of my soul. It was at that moment that I realized I had been running from him for so long. Something dark inside was instantly broken. My guilt and shame and sin seemed to be lifted from me like a giant crane lifting the collapsed rubble of an imploded building. I was forgiven! I was debt free! I felt alive and flooded with joy on the inside. A smile broke out on my face. It was a smile like I've never smiled before. Here I was behind metal bars and cinderblock walls, yet I felt freer than I had felt in my entire life. Outside of these walls without Jesus I had been in a prison that I could not escape, but now I was free inside these towering confines. Jesus had set me free. My heart wanted to fly.

Vince and Tad were of course thrilled for me. Vince invited me to the prison church at 7:30 on Tuesday night. It was great and became the highlight of my week. Soon things seemed to speed up, and I found myself marveling at what was taking place. It seemed that once I asked God to come into my life, he started working like never before.

One week later I was moved to Arrowhead Correctional Center to complete phase two of my treatment program. I couldn't believe it when they transferred Vince with me and assigned him as my cellmate. God was truly orchestrating things in my life. I was given the highest paying job in prison, making over one hundred fifty dollars per month working in the greenhouse as a daisy grower. Phase two treatment was very intensive, with work for four hours a day and the rest of the day spent in classes. But the good news was I had better visitation privileges. My wife and children soon came up to see me, and we enjoyed the hours of just being together. I bubbled over trying to share what had happened. My wife just listened quietly, her face breaking into a gentle smile that spoke volumes. For the first time in my whole life,

I had hope. Something we had never experienced together before began to emerge, slowly replacing the dismal place of despair. Jesus had restored hope.

Then a new curve ball came flying over the plate. Two days after the visit of my wife and children, we were told that a new ruling had been made. Sex offenders were no longer allowed to visit with their children. They were sorry, but this would be the rule from here on out. I was devastated. After collecting my thoughts from the disappointing news, I decided to talk to God about it. "Lord, I don't understand this. It seemed like you were working to reconnect me with my family and things were going well, and now this. I am praying that you will help me see my kids."

The very next day while working my job, the case manager called me to the office. "Matt, you are being transferred to a halfway house in Fort Collins. Your wife and kids can visit you there." God had intervened and come to my aid. I couldn't believe it. I knew I did not deserve his favor, but he was pouring it out on me. I felt loved by him. It was a love that I had never known before, and it was real. I was getting out of prison! It had been three years since I had left the courtroom to do my time. It seemed like another life ago. That day I thanked God with everything I had in me. I looked up at the sky and, with tears streaming down my cheeks, said out loud, "Lord, I believe you more now than I did three weeks ago! You are all powerful, all knowing, and all loving!"

My life during this time seemed covered in love. At least that is how I felt. God had broken into the deepest, darkest part of my heart and spoken his love. His love had taken me where I needed to go. I wouldn't take back one day. I needed to go to prison so he could reach my heart. It was in prison that I finally was truly broken. I came to a place where I gave in and didn't want to run any longer. I didn't want to fight any more. My own hell on earth and bondage to addiction was more than I could bear. I needed someone stronger than me to set me free. And that someone was Jesus Christ. He loved me when I couldn't even love myself. His love changed my heart, gave me a reason to live, and set me free to a new life, even behind prison bars. His love also destroyed the shackles of my addiction. The beast was slain. The oppressive power of the dark obsession within my heart was defeated. I could not do it through my own strength or determination. I could not escape it through denial. I could not do enough penance to pay for it. Only Jesus has the power to forgive me and set me free. His love is relentless; it's tenacious. He pursued me into the stone walls of prison. My heart overflows with gratitude still.

CHAPTER EIGHT

Freedom of Forgiveness

The Dilemma

On the day of the event as I sat on the curb outside my home speaking with Matt, the words came blurting out of my mouth, "I forgive you." They were words uttered in a moment of shock. Later, as I was driving to my husband's office they came back to me with full force. What had I done? What had I said? Was it the right thing? Was it real?

A struggle began to take shape in my heart. Someone had entered my world with the intent to inflict great pain, probably even death. He had invaded my space with a deadly weapon and had brought great trauma to me, and my family. What was I doing, saying that I had forgiven him so soon? Maybe this would give him the message that what had been done was no big deal. Maybe he would think I was quick to brush off the assault because it had little effect on me. And what about consequences? Did forgiveness negate the need to report this to the police? What would other women say when they found out I had forgiven my assailant after he had threatened me in such a violent way? Would they feel that I had betrayed womanhood and the cause of many females who had found themselves victimized at the hands of a brutal man?

A myriad of questions continued to swirl through my thoughts. What was forgiveness anyway? What commitment was I making? What responsibilities did it carry? Sorting all of this through was no easy task, but something inside of me kept pressing forward as if to say in a prodding, relentless voice, "Where you settle on this issue matters."

I had been a believer in Jesus Christ for all of my life and had been raised to know him and trust him. Because of this I was very familiar with the subject of forgiveness. I had grown up being told that God forgives me and there is nothing I cannot bring to him. As a young girl I was taught Scriptures, such as the one that says, "If we confess our sins, he is faithful and just and will forgive us our sins and purify us from all unrighteousness."[17] My parents taught me that God was full of grace and love, and when I had done wrong I could come to him, confess, and find his pardon. Not only did they instruct me in the ways of God, they lived them out themselves. I had been fortunate enough to grow up in a family that embraced grace and forgiveness as a way of life. We weren't perfect by any standard. But those values were alive in our midst. I just didn't realize how much they had become a part of me.

It was out of the profound sense of God's forgiveness for me that I found in my heart a desire to forgive Matt. Over the thirty-eight years of my life, I had known the bountiful freedom that comes with forgiveness. Memories flooded my conscience of times I had wounded others deeply or betrayed the trust of a friend with an outright lie. But the memory of my sin began to blur and fade as I realized the extent of his grace and mercy in forgiveness, and I felt the weight of the world lifted from my shoulders.

With these thoughts in mind I knew that I wanted to forgive Matt, so he too would know the healing balm of pardon. But what about justice? Surely I couldn't push aside the enormity of what had just taken place. What would prevent Matt from repeating this crime with me or someone else when he was released from prison? Was forgiveness premature? Was my first response a hopelessly naïve position?

Pursuing the answers to these questions helped me begin to understand what forgiveness is not, especially in the days following the traumatic events that had just taken place. First, I realized that forgiveness did not condone or diminish Matt's behavior. What he had done was devastating and evil. Nothing could whitewash the facts. He had intended great harm, and he could do the same again. Next time the results could be deadly. No, the crime had to be called what it was: a destructive, malevolent act. Forgiveness does not redefine evil.

Second, it became clear that forgiveness does not necessarily eliminate consequences. I had reported the crime to the police, and they had sent detectives out to my home to investigate the story. There was no attempt on my part to soften the account or pull back from the truth of what had taken place. Matt had been arrested and the consequences of the law soon descended upon him. I didn't demand or insist on any agenda, but reported the story and let things unfold in the light of truth.

Third, I also realized that forgiveness does not depend on whether or not the offender is truly sorry. Matt had repeatedly said, "I'm sorry," both on the curb just after the attack and in subsequent letters to our residence. I believed that he truly had a measure of sorrow. Maybe he was sorry that things had not gone according to plan. Maybe he was sorry that he had been derailed and was now facing a sea of hot water. I was sure that things looked pretty bleak from Matt's perspective, and he was probably sorry about that. Down deep, however, I knew there was more that was happening in him. I believed that God was working on Matt, even though I knew nothing of where he was or what was going on in his life. Only God knew what Matt truly needed for full restoration and heart transformation. I didn't have to figure out if he was really sorry. I never had to be his judge in order to forgive him. There was a tangible sense of relief knowing that this was all in God's hands, not mine.

As I worked through unpredictable emotions and wrestled with new realities, I started to realize what forgiveness did mean. It meant I was choosing to release Matt from any debt to me. I didn't have to use up valuable energy and time to make sure he paid his dues and received his just penalty. I didn't have to be consumed with his punishment, tied up with desire for revenge, fretful that the authorities would handle things poorly, anxious that he would get let off the hook, or worried that he would work the system. I could place all of this—and Matt himself—into the hands of God. God, who is a God of justice, would do what was right. Didn't the Bible confirm this when it says, "Do not repay anyone evil for evil," and, "Do not take revenge, my dear friends, but leave room for God's wrath, for it is written: 'It is mine to avenge; I will repay,' says the Lord."[18] If there was avenging that needed to be done, then God was very capable to take care of it. And I had to admit, being avenged by God was not something any sane person would choose. I found my own heart again filled with compassion for Matt. Down deep I wanted him to be dealt with mercifully, and continued to pray that God would intervene in his life.

Because of this, one week later, I was able to write as part of a letter to Matt the words, "By God's grace, I forgive you." Those words were real. I knew that I meant it. God's grace had given me the ability to choose to forgive. It was a choice that I was making even though at the time I didn't fully understand its enormity. That day when I resolved to forgive I had no idea of where that forgiveness would take me or where it would take Matt. I had little knowledge of the explosion of events that the choice would ignite. I couldn't even begin to imagine that day the blessings that would flow into my life and Matt's through just this one decision. It was a decision that changed my life and his.

A New Revelation

Not too long after this time I read a book by Philip Yancey entitled *What's So Amazing About Grace?* The book was in itself a small part of the grace awakening that was happening in my own life and in others at the time. The chapter on forgiveness was profound for me. Yancey stated, "We remain bound to the people we cannot forgive, held in their vise grip."[19] How true! It would not have been hard to remain connected to this horrific event in my life. I knew that unforgiveness would keep me tied to the emotions and entanglement of the trauma, and I would be trapped in a stagnant place of resentment and bitterness. Unforgiveness would attach me permanently to my perpetrator and weave me into a web of dysfunction. Unforgiveness would hold me hostage even though God had worked for my release by providing a way of escape out my front door. It was a tie that I needed broken if I was going to move forward and heal. Yancey's words again rang true, "Not to forgive imprisons me in the past and locks out all potential for change."[20] God had provided the way forward: the way of forgiveness.

Then I read words that proved to be pure gold to me. In front of me on a page in Yancey's book were words that brought a visual I couldn't deny or ignore. He said, "When we genuinely forgive, we set a prisoner free and then discover that the prisoner we set free was us."[21] That was it! Matt was in jail, locked up behind bars. Yet I too could find myself in the same place of bondage and confinement even though my bars were unseen. Unforgiveness would create its own prison, and I would be locked behind its doors missing out on the joy of life. But it was not to be. Forgiveness would set me free. It wasn't dependent on Matt's remorse or my own feelings. It was ultimately rooted in the forgiveness of God, and it was a choice I could make with his strength and by his grace. It was a choice that allowed God to do what God does best—work out all things for good in the context of his justice and love. I could trust that he would do just that. I could move forward in his freedom with the weight off my shoulders. I just wanted to shout for joy. He had given me his own heart for Matt and had given me a desire to forgive. What I didn't fully realize at the time was the great benefit this was to me as well. It's the gift that continues to unfold its riches with time. God was offering me the key to my cell, dangling it on the end of the golden chain of his love. He says, "My child, I have forgiven you. Now go and forgive others. In this you will find freedom." Well, that is my paraphrase of Colossians 3:13.

While the choice to forgive takes place in a moment, I discovered that following through on the decision is a process. My thinking changed, and daily I learned to give my need to control back to God. I could trust him to work things out. I could trust that he would do what was right for my life. The healing could take place when I was liberated from my past trauma.

Throughout the years following the encounter with Matt, God continued to teach me about forgiveness, a core component in an abundant and full life. I marveled anew as I read through the account of Christ's suffering and deep anguish on a Roman cross. I couldn't think of a greater evil that could be perpetrated.

Murdering God. Rejecting, spitting upon, torturing, and mocking deity. Abusing, piercing, and shaming one who had done no wrong. Why didn't God the Father say, "Enough of you all!" and rain fire down from the sky obliterating the whole ugly mess? Why didn't Jesus seethe with anger at his assailants, and then in a moment of retaliation, speak to the earth to open up and swallow the whole lot of them? It certainly would have been justified. It probably wouldn't have surprised too many in the heavenly courts.

Jesus again shocked onlookers by operating outside the confines of the human imagination. His kingdom wasn't of this world, and he chose to respond in a way that turned us all upside down. During his lifetime men had stood in awe. When anger was expected, he responded with compassion. When judgment was the normal response, he gave grace. When scarcity was the rule of thumb, he produced abundance. Now as he hung dying he would exceed every expectation, rupture every preconceived idea, and shatter every human anticipation. Instead of using his power on the group that flanked his cross, he let them have their way. He appeared to be giving in to their evil and destructive plot. Had he run out of fight? Why didn't he save himself and destroy those who dared to mock? Those who knew him well knew he could.

I found myself entering into the story, standing there in person. It was as if I was in the gawking crowd. All eyes were on him as the moments of his life moved to a close. Certainly at any time, he would rise up and mete out justice. Any time now. Yet out of his mouth came words that I am still trying to comprehend today. "Father, forgive them, for they do not know what they are doing."[222] Forgive. Where did *that* come from? It came from the heart of God. A heart of incomprehensible love and mercy.

My heart began to melt as I realized I was the recipient of this wondrous, indescribable, incomprehensible love. He was talking to me that day. He was forgiving me. The reality of this forgiveness broke through the deepest place in my heart. I felt humbled by this story. I had been forgiven so much. How could I withhold the same gift from Matt? If Jesus could forgive such a horrific assault to himself, surely I could forgive Matt.

Forgiving Matt didn't mean reconciliation. I didn't need to have a relationship with him to forgive him. That was not possible. I just needed to release any expectation of debt. He owed me nothing. Forgiving Matt did not depend on me forgetting what had taken place, either. I remembered the trauma of the day far too well. But something extraordinary had happened. Even though I remembered the events of the assault, they no longer worked inside to hurt me. It was like they were reframed. I knew what had happened. I wasn't in denial. But instead of the event bringing memories of fear and trepidation, I was reminded of God's faithful hand and how he had brought comfort to my heart and used the experience to draw me closer to himself. I saw God holding me instead of a man accosting me.

Forgiving Matt didn't mean that some kind of trust was restored with him. Only God knew his heart, and God was taking him on the journey he needed to travel. I could trust this. My job was to pray for him and his family and know that God was working in a place I could not see. My heart was being changed toward him in the process. I could honestly say that my hope for him was that he would find the peace, strength, healing, and redemption that God had for him. Something inside of me kept telling me that someday my prayers could very well be answered.

In the meantime God had more work to do in me. I began to wonder if there were others in my life that I needed to forgive. What was holding me back or keeping me tied to the past? Periodically God would reveal a place in my heart that harbored resentment or bitterness. My journey had made an impact. I no longer wanted any fragment of darkness there. The sooner it was released the better off I knew I would be. In the years following the event my own heart went through a good housecleaning. It was timely and restoring.

Part of the purging in me had to do with taking offense. I couldn't find a single instance where Jesus was personally offended by someone and put his guard up in defense. It just didn't happen. While he defended his Father's glory and temple with vigor and even a show of righteous anger, he never seemed to allow the mistreatment and insults of others towards himself to find their mark. He never retaliated or pouted. He never snubbed or rejected. He seemed to rise above the offense, loving and praying for the offenders. And, the truth is, dying for them. It brought back a Scripture that I had posted on my bedroom door long ago during my high school days. It was a modern version of 1 Corinthians 13, and I still remember the words that have stuck with me all these years, "Love doesn't notice when others do it wrong." I vowed to be that kind of person. I prayed that I would refuse offense, and love instead. Only with his help would it be possible.

The Secret Ingredient

As I look back on this time in my life, I discovered a profound truth: Forgiveness was the secret ingredient to my healing. It wasn't just saying the words, "I forgive you," even though those words are important. It was learning to walk in forgiveness, to let the words take root in my life, and to live in the reality of those words. I learned to embrace God's all-encompassing forgiveness in my own life, and then to respond in humble gratitude. God was teaching me that gratitude could be a way of life, but it was easily pushed aside by the bully of unforgiveness. That bully was ruthless when he was allowed into school. When the bully was expelled, then gratitude returned and flourished.

When I had stood in the courtroom on April 4, 1996 and read my statement, there was a message I wanted to give. The written statement ended with these words: "I want Matt to know that he is loved by God and forgiven by me." My ability to forgive was ultimately rooted in the love and forgiveness of God. The prisoner had been set free, and it was me. Some days I found myself weeping in gratitude. At times my heart could not contain the overwhelming release in it all.

Time passed, and the season of pastoral ministry that began in 1998 brought new insights into forgiveness. In the summer of 2005 a young woman walked into my office with a question: Would the church be willing to sponsor some kind of addiction recovery program? This began a new adventure of learning and discovery that I could never have anticipated.

One year later we launched Celebrate Recovery, a Christ-centered recovery program based on principles found in the words of Jesus. Since I was the pastor overseeing the program, I stepped in with two feet. I just wasn't prepared for how much it would impact me personally. Many flooded through the doors looking for hope and help—those addicted to meth, alcohol, pornography, prescription drugs, or hurtful relationships. Others came who had suffered from eating disorders, abuse, incest, or violence and were filled with shame and humiliation.

God met us all there. Over time many found restored hope and new life. Addictions were broken and hearts were healed. Those I was surrounded with became my friends, and I learned how much we had in common. We were all trying to navigate our way through life and all very much in need of the grace of God.

Even though I didn't struggle with the same things as others, I had my struggles. They just had different names. I learned that I had a tendency to try to manage things on my own, and often fell into the trappings of the cultural message of autonomy, independence, and individualism.

While God had worked to lift me out of the place of immobilizing fear, I realized that there was another rut on the other side of the street to fall into. That rut was one of overconfidence, failing to realize how much I need the strength, wisdom, and provision of God every day of my life. I learned my greatest flaw was a relentless self-dependency and the need to be seen as one who could skillfully keep all the plates spinning. The trouble was, behind the scenes I knew I was failing at keeping it all together and the plates were crashing. No matter how hard I tried, it seemed I kept falling short. The self-disclosure that followed was painful but freeing.

The most painful part, I think, was admitting my struggle when I had been accustomed to tucking it away where I thought no one would see. It was hard to be vulnerable with the others around me, fearing perhaps that they may see me differently or think less of me. As a pastor I enthusiastically embraced my role of helping others through their struggles. But share mine? Even though I knew that my Celebrate Recovery family was a safe place, I still wondered if they would think me less capable to fulfill my ministry role should they know that underneath the confident exterior was one who often became overwhelmed, discouraged, and just plain tired.

The day I shared my deep challenges and struggles with trusted comrades was the day I made a grand discovery. My issue did not shock them or even surprise them. What I thought was hidden from their sight was really in full view. They already knew, and they loved me anyway. In fact, many shared that they, too, struggled with the same things. Again, it was reinforced to me that *everyone* has *something* they struggle with. A wonderful freedom began to take shape in my heart. No matter the issue, we all benefited from walking this journey together, encouraging each other, holding each other accountable, supporting each other, and praying for one another. In this environment we were all becoming better people, and God was able to work mighty things in our lives.

When I realized that I could confess my faults to another trusted person, as well as to God, I felt the pressure come off. I didn't have to keep up the façade of having it all together. I learned that many women (as well as men) shared in my malady. Our culture gives messages that tell us we have to do it all to be a good mom, a faithful wife, or a competent female. And we really do try. But sooner or later it comes crashing down because we are humanly unable to keep up with the magnitude of the demand.

Scripture came to mind, and I framed it and hung it in my office. It is God's words to his people found in Isaiah and says, "In repentance and rest is your salvation, in quietness and trust is your strength, but you would have none of it."[23] I learned that I didn't have to take myself so seriously and I could admit my shortcomings and rely on trusted others. I didn't have to take it all on. It was okay to say *no*. I also learned that my identity wasn't defined by what I accomplished; rather it was defined by whose I was—a beloved daughter of God. He was calling me to repentance and rest, internal quietness and trust. This gave me a freedom to slow down and to be fully present in the rich moments of my life. It also gave me the courage to step into new arenas without the fear of failure immobilizing me, or the need for affirmation driving me.

My time working through the recovery program taught me about the high value of surrender and walking in humble dependence on God. I learned that placing trust in the provision and power of Jesus was the strongest place I could choose to be.

Core to all of recovery is the issue of forgiveness. We learned that the inability to forgive could block, stall, or destroy the journey to freedom and that forgiveness is God's prescription for the broken. It became clear that no matter how great the offense or abuse, forgiveness lies on the path to wholeness—both giving it and receiving it. Denial isn't an option, neither is blame, excuse, or buried pain. Responding to the lists we made of people we needed to forgive, as well as people we needed to make amends to, was a step in the journey to peace and freedom.

Forgiveness. Flowing from the heart of God. Rooted in his abundant love. It sets the prisoners free. It gives the bound new life. The debt is canceled and the payment made. When I started to get it, the joy and gratitude flowed over me like a cascading spring in a desert. One of my favorite psalms says it all, "For as high as the heavens are above the earth, so great is his love for those who fear him; as far as the east is from the west, so far has he removed our transgressions from us. As a father has compassion on his children, so the LORD has compassion on those who fear him."[24]

I thought back to that day in July 1998. I had experienced the love and forgiveness of God. I longed for Matt to know the same. I didn't have any idea where he was or what he was doing. All I knew was that he had been sentenced to six years and faced the confines of a difficult prison term. I could only trust that the God of love was doing everything in his power to break through with his message of grace and hope. Matt and I stood on level ground at the foot of the cross. Both in need of the love, mercy, and forgiveness of God. Would Matt open his heart to the pardon offered to him? He was in prison doing time but not outside of the reach of God. Would Matt choose life?

Swinging the door open, I bustled into my home carrying an armload of groceries. The afternoon had been busy, and I needed to catch up. Going over to the answering machine I pushed the button on the front of the box to check messages. A soft voice caught my attention, and the words I heard caused me to stop short. "Rose, this is Matt's wife. I want you to know that because of this experience in your home both Matt and I have received Jesus Christ as Savior and Lord. I just thought you should know. Goodbye."

CHAPTER NINE

Breaking the Chains

Freedom and Fear

As I rode into Fort Collins in the Department of Corrections van, I realized it had been years since I had been in a vehicle. We were going eighty miles an hour, and it scared me to see things flying by so fast. I started noticing the colorful clothing that people were wearing, like a new and intriguing novelty of another culture. Children were playing, people were laughing, life was everywhere, abounding. I felt like I had been reborn. It occurred to me that God was using the experience of what I had gone through to show me what life in him is like. It is truly a rebirth to a new life!

Soon my wife and children came for a visit. It was wonderful, because now I was only a thirty-minute drive away. We sat next to each other, eating lunch together, and hugged and kissed as much as we wanted. I could hardly believe what was happening. This was only one week after I had been told that I couldn't see my kids! My love for God continued to grow. He was daily showing me his faithfulness.

Within the first ten days I was hired in a woodshop doing what I loved and making more money than I had in my life outside of prison. I was able to get a bus pass to travel back and forth from work to the halfway house. Before long, I was supervising thirteen other men, and my boss was pleased with me. At times it all seemed surreal. It is funny what you appreciate when you don't have it any longer. Eating with metal silverware became quite a treat after years with plastic forks. I also found great joy in playing my guitar. I had built it just before I entered prison, and my wife was able to bring it to me in the halfway house. In the evenings I spent hours just strumming its taut strings and letting the rich harmony sink into my being.

While it was evident that good things were happening in my life, the halfway house presented its own set of challenges. In many ways, some of my greatest hardships and most severe mental temptations would happen at this place. This was a whole new world from what I had known for the last three and a half years.

I began to reflect back on my oppressive prison journey and noticed that I had seen the hand of God even in the midst of darkness and pain. I did not notice his intervention at the time, but it came into clear view as I looked back. He had placed Raymond in my life. Our friendship began in the detention center and continued on through the hellish events of Park County. Had not Raymond intervened, I surely would have killed someone. The thought horrified me. He was the best buddy I could have had. He stuck with me, and together we survived. Looking back I knew he had been a gift from God—a rugged, tough, sharp-tongued gift from God.

God had brought me through the ordeal and kept me sane. He was there working for me even when I didn't know who he was. In the midst of the devastation I had made of my life, he showed up and worked in remarkable ways to rescue me from the destruction to which I was headed.

I also received some bits of news that brought a sense of closure to a portion of the horrors that I had experienced. First, a young boy who had been sentenced to Park County Detention Center had been released and informed his attorney father of the evil and intense corruption going on in that place. It was shut down by the state soon after I had been moved on. Second, I received a letter from Raymond. He had met up with Jack, who wanted to apologize for the escalating violence he had initiated with me. His heart had been devastated by the news of his wife's abandonment, and he exploded. I was the one nearby that took the shrapnel of his anger. Now he wanted reconciliation for a long ago offense. Of course. He was a good man down deep.

Coming to the halfway house had been a huge step forward for me. For the first time in my whole life I had hope. It had begun when I found Jesus in prison. At the same time, a new and profound fear began taking hold of my insides in a very deep and insidious way. From the time of my sentence to the present I had been behind bars, and in a peculiar sort of way they had provided a measure of security for me. When the tormenting thoughts had returned during my incarceration, and the urges of the addiction became unbearable, I was restrained from acting them out. I began to feel a sense of safety behind the barricades and a feeling of comfort at my imposed imprisonment. At least I couldn't carry out my deviant desires. I began to place an abnormal trust in my confinement.

But something had changed inside me when I finally surrendered to God and openly confessed my belief in Jesus. I had not experienced one of those driving compulsions since. I wanted to believe that God had truly set me free. But could he keep me free? What would happen now in the "real world"? Would I succumb again to the beast within now that I was outside of my protective barriers? Could I stand up to the onslaught of temptation on the outside of the prison walls? The fear inside began to mount. I knew that I didn't have the ability in my own strength to keep from sliding backwards and eventually ending up back in prison. Little did I know the magnitude of the battle I was soon to face.

When I first arrived at the halfway house, I enjoyed three-hour passes to visit with my wife and children. This was a piece of heaven for me, and I drank in every moment like a thirsty man. It was what I lived for. But my joy was short lived. Just a few days into my new residence, I was informed that I would no longer be allowed to see my children. I was a registered sex offender, and the rules had been toughened. Even though my victim had been an adult, the authorities were concerned about crossover behavior.

I was back in regular treatment with a licensed therapist who knew that my urgent goal was to get back home with my wife and kids. Out of sheer frustration I probed, "Am I ever going to be able to move back home?" All my therapist could offer was an emotionless shrug. Discouragement flooded over me. I had come this far, and now an impenetrable wall seemed to stand in my path. My dream of seeing my wife and kids shattered.

Just as I was beginning to slump into a place of despair, another thought came bombarding into my mind, much like Raymond had done years ago when he intercepted a potentially lethal fight. "God has gotten you this far. He isn't going to fail you now. If he brought you here, then he has the power to take you to the goal of your journey: home. He can get you through this seemingly impossible roadblock. You just need to do the next right thing." God had intercepted a potentially lethal mindset. I just needed to keep going.

Soon my therapist worked out a plan, and I was able to travel across town to a halfway house to see my wife and kids. After being able to visit with them freely at first, I now had to comply with limited supervised visits. But with disappointment and determination, I accepted what was offered, appreciating any time I had with my family.

Since I wasn't allowed to have a driver's license, I purchased a bicycle and rode it everywhere I had to go. I figured out, without exaggeration, that I was riding an average of a hundred and sixty-eight miles per week. Each morning I got up at four and rode to the east side of town for work. Winter days were no exception, arriving at work after cautiously navigating the narrow tires through icy patches and drizzling snow. After a ten-hour day of work I would ride back to the halfway house, do my chores, and then ride several hours to the location for my daily sex-offender treatment. Following the two-hour-long treatment, I rode back again to the halfway house, then biked the twelve-mile roundtrip to the Harmony House to see my family.

Initially it was a frustrating arrangement, but I was so grateful for the opportunity that I rode my heart out without complaint. There were some side benefits too. I had always hated my chicken legs and tried to hide them under long trousers. Now when I looked down at the once-feeble knees, I saw that I had some pretty good muscles developing. But most importantly, I got to see my kids. Everything I was doing was worth it. I was learning to be grateful for what I had and thanked God for all that he was giving me, even if it meant hard work. Even though it was arduous and challenging, I never griped, complained, or moaned about what I had to do.

One day I was given the privilege of eating with my family at a restaurant near the halfway house. In order to do this I had to bike the six miles to meet them at the Harmony House, then bike back into town another six miles to meet them for dinner. My family would drive the car to meet me since we weren't allowed to ride in a vehicle together. We had enjoyed a great visit, and I was now heading for dinner, pumping my bike for all I was worth to make it there on time. In my strenuous haste, I hit a curb going about thirty-five miles per hour and immediately took a headfirst plunge over the handlebars, landing on my back on the concrete. In the blow, my knees had buckled up toward my face, and I lay on the ground, writhing with intense pain. I thought I had shattered my back.

Turns out the passerby who called the ambulance thought the same thing. The paramedics arrived and insisted I go to the ER for treatment, but I couldn't bear the thought of missing my kids at dinner. With a trembling hand I signed the waiver to refuse service, and, in agony, climbed back on my bike to pedal back to the halfway house and then to dinner. Going to the hospital was not an option, and being late was not an option either. I just had to keep going. I couldn't take a chance on jeopardizing this time with my family, so I rode as fast as my legs would go. My lungs struggled to take in a breath because everything hurt so bad.

Tears from pain were streaming down my face while we were eating that night, but I made it happen. Determination had won out. I was with my kids. It took some time for my body to recover, but I had my sights set on the goal. All I was going through was worth it.

Several months into the halfway house I made a request to go to church, and after meeting with the pastor and explaining my situation, it was approved. The good part was they didn't make me ride my bike! My family could pick me up. We went to the church where my wife had found the Lord while I was in prison. I was glad she picked such a good one with a kind and gracious pastor. This time became really important to me, and I did everything I could to never miss a service, finding my heart swelling inside as I sat alongside my three children and my wife. This was a dream come true.

However, things had been tough at the halfway house. The first day that I arrived, I walked out of the front door to find one of the other male residents standing on top the picnic table in the front yard. He was straining to peer over the fence and yelled with enthusiasm, "Hey, check this out!" I soon learned that our state-assigned home was next door to a sorority. In fact there were four sorority houses within a block. We were all sex offenders who were supposed to be recovering, yet temptations were literally next door.

Sometimes I would come home to find the guys staring and cheering as the college girls in the houses adjacent to us undressed in front of windows with the drapes open, oblivious to the commotion that was being stirred next door. All of this gripped my heart with pure fear. I was scared because I didn't know if I was strong yet. How could the powers that be let this happen? It all seemed so wrong. The system placed so much emphasis on protecting my children, yet they threw me in the middle of a bunch of half-dressed beautiful women.

The other thing that shocked me was that the halfway house was coed. Not long after I arrived, one of the female residents propositioned me. I soon learned that guys and girls were getting together all the time, hidden away in the many nooks and isolated rooms of the old house. I never participated in the seductive activities, but it made me scared and angry. How was I supposed to get past this addiction when I was surrounded with things that were trying to draw me back into the same old place? When I mentioned the situation to a friend, he got angry too. The system that was supposed to be helping me just seemed so broken much of the time. I finally had to tell him, "Your anger isn't helping me at all. I'm doing everything I can *not* to be angry and frustrated." None of us had the power or desire to renovate the system. We just wanted to do our time and be out.

That's when I knew this was my responsibility. I couldn't depend on being confined behind prison bars to do the right thing. I couldn't place my confidence in being assigned to a house away from all temptation in order to make right choices. I couldn't trust that someone or something else was going to protect me from wrong behavior. I had to make those decisions. There were things all around me that seemed to be lurking in the shadows, ready to jump out and ensnare me in the grip of self-destruction, and I knew I had to be alert. I never looked at the sorority girls. But I was scared. I was really scared. I was back out in society now, and I didn't know if God had completely taken this lust and sexual addiction away from me yet. I was young in my faith and new to this Christian life. Was I strong? Could I resist or would I be pulled back down into the bottomless cavern of emptiness, pain, and driving lust that had consumed me before?

Two things at this time became my lifeline: my Bible and my guitar. Every day I read a scripture or two and carried it with me to think about all through the day. These small nuggets had greater impact on me than I realized at the time. Through them God was changing me, one verse at a time, as they became part of my way of thinking. The guitar I had was one that I had built myself before I went to prison. When I saw my wife walk through the door with my prized instrument in her hand, my heart sprang to new life with the anticipation of playing songs and filling the old halfway house with music. Music was God's tool for breaking into the deep places of my heart.

It was about this time that I realized something new. It wasn't there—the old thing, the tormenting addiction, the consuming thoughts. They were gone. I was in the midst of attractive women, but my thoughts were on my wife and how I would get to see her and my children at church on Sunday. What God had begun, he was now taking me through the process of cementing. Hope again took hold of my heart.

Reflecting on my life, I could see the destructive effect of pornography. It is so accepted in the culture that most people don't give it a second thought. I know I didn't. It bombards us from every angle, and it is easy to think it is harmless. But it was anything but harmless for me. It was the crude images and tantalizing photos that worked as a seed in my young heart for the destructive path that followed. It insidiously took hold of my mind without me realizing it. The deceptive trap of this shallow stimulator robbed me of having healthy thoughts about sex. It stole from my ability to truly enjoy and love my wife. Oh, if only I could have another chance.

The images were no longer tormenting me and seemed to be gone. Once I needed them to get my fix after a big life-disappointment. But now that need was no longer there. God had taken it from me. I knew I could choose to stay clear of vulgar materials and keep my thoughts on things that were good and right. With God's help I would trust that the images would stay gone. I longed for nothing more than to return to my wife with a new heart that could really love her as she deserved to be loved.

Walking out the Freedom

Nine months went by in the halfway house, and then one day I received the news. I was approved to be released on parole. Initially my heart was ecstatic. It was really happening! After four years away from my family, it was really happening. I had been engrossed in trying to do everything well. I attended group therapy meetings two nights a week for two hours each night, worked hard, obeyed the rules, cooperated with all the regulations, and pretty much immersed myself in doing the right thing. My sights were set on the goal: getting home with my family. I was surely ready now. But then the hammer dropped, and it dropped hard. No sex offender from the Department of Corrections was allowed to go home if minor children resided in the house.

My prayer intensity increased. My wife prayed. We pleaded with God and bargained with him. "Please, Lord, please find a way to get me home. It seems like the right thing. You know I love my children, Lord. Please just make it happen." Again, my caseworker could only shrug.

All my hard work seemed for naught. I had excelled in my treatment program and kept my nose to the grindstone. I was so close to my goal and just couldn't get there. After being released from the halfway house, I wasn't allowed to go home. The law prevented me because my children were still young. I understood the risk that my supervisory team would be making to let me live with my family but that didn't curb the disappointment. The only option was finding an inexpensive place to live. I began to search, but my heart felt flat.

The apartment I rented was nice with two bedrooms and a washer and dryer. It had everything I needed and seemed a good deal for what I could afford. I walked in the first evening and took a deep breath as I surveyed the stark interior. Might as well make the best of whatever I was given. Moving toward the window I opened the curtain to survey the view. What caught my eyes took my breath away. The old wooden structure next door was a college party house and the open window was no more than fifteen feet away. There in full view was a couple in the throes of lovemaking.

Fear gripped me again. I didn't know what to do with it. Why did this keep happening? I didn't need this! A few days later I looked out the window on the other side of the room to discover that the view was right into the bathroom of the house next door, complete with showering coeds. Everywhere I turned it seemed that there were college kids who were in the midst of a carefree life with little concern for privacy or modesty. I didn't want to be there!

I was trying to come out of addiction, yet it seemed that there was another force at work. God had done a miracle in my life, but it felt like there was a concerted effort in some unseen realm to snag me again and drag me back into the old place. It was uncanny. It was like someone or something knew exactly where my weak spot had been, and I was being barraged with temptations specifically designed to take me down. These encounters were just too frequent to be happenchance. In many respects it felt like the county detention center all over again. I had a sense that everything swirling around me was out of control and beyond figuring out.

But God was not going to let go of me now. Somehow he allowed me to see behind the scenes and begin to understand what I was going through. I was in a battle. There was a battle for my very soul. My enemy is real and his intent is my destruction. He was successful before and had been forced to relinquish his hold. He would not give up easily. I had once been his property, and he had full control of my life. He surely wasn't happy with my new change of direction. Right now it felt like there was an all-out effort to retrieve me and bring me back into the enemy's fold. I know now it was spiritual warfare. All I could feel at the time, however, was just the war.

What seemed to compound the difficulty during this time was that I felt so alone. I couldn't talk to anyone about the onslaught I was facing on a daily basis. My group wouldn't understand, and my parole officer would immediately want to get me out. This would be quite difficult with the year lease that I had signed. So I turned to the only one I had, one who was new for me—God. I prayed in a new way, seeking his help to stay strong and to persevere, asking him to keep my heart focused and true, and trusting him to give me the strength to resist the detrimental pulls around me. I could see he was coming through. Each day I felt a little stronger.

Continuing in a positive track felt good. I was going to church with my family and enjoying the small segments of time that I could be with them. Soon I received word that my wife could come to spend the night once a week. This was monumental. I had not been able to be intimate with my wife for four and a half years, and I treasured this time as a gift beyond description. Months later I was granted weekend passes to go home for a couple of days. What a milestone! I couldn't live at home but I could stay for a while. I knew this meant I was on track for my dreams to be fulfilled. My heart soared with praise to God. It had been a lot of hard work, but getting home is what I lived for. It felt like nothing could stop me because I was focused, and I had the Lord on my side.

Finally at the end of a year in my apartment, when the lease was up, I received the word for which I had been waiting for many years. I could move home! Because of my good behavior they had taken a risk on me. I could go home with my minor children. A rush of overwhelming gratitude flooded over me as the news sunk in. The tears began to flow, and my heart felt as if it would just rupture and lay in a puddle at my feet. I was going home! It wasn't long before I was consumed with a new thought of almost incomprehensible magnitude: I had a home to go to. My wife had stuck it out with me through this nightmare of my own choices. She hadn't given up or left. She was there to welcome me back. My children had persevered through the devastation of a father in prison. They had loved me through it all and emotionally supported my journey. How did I deserve such a blessing? I was humbled beyond words. Down deep I knew that I would not have found the strength to go on if my family had exited my life. But they were here, and I would never, ever cease from thanking God for them.

From the time I had left the state prison, I had been blessed with good jobs making significant salary. My creative construction and woodworking skills proved valuable, landing me jobs in cabinet shops, woodworking industries, and high-end window production. But now I needed a job close to home. It was the final thing to get me back to my life. After approval from my parole officer, I quickly landed a job in a high-end woodworking corporation and knew I had completed the journey home. It had been a long road to move home.

Walking up the cracked cement walkway and through the front door, knowing that I was going to stay, was a feeling that defies description. No words are adequate for what was going on in my heart. God had brought me through. I had been on a road to self-destruction, and he had plucked me out of the pit and taken me on a journey to restore my life. The gratitude flowed out through the tears that filled my eyes. My new life was beginning. Just getting my driver's license again after so long was pure joy. So was the new car we were able to purchase. We had never lived like this before!

The joy was surreal, yet life brought realities with it in the months to follow. Deep down I knew that God had performed a miracle in my life. Finally, it was real! I had been freed from my lethal addiction. However, I knew I couldn't be cocky, self-assured, or flippant about the freedom that had been purchased at so great a cost. I could make choices that would bring my bondage back again—and in full force the next time. Going back to that place sent shivers down my spine. It was clear that I had been granted a reprieve, but I had to cooperate with the gift of freedom I had been given. I needed to do what God wanted me to do. And he was giving me the strength to do it.

Looking back I realized that God had taken me on an incredible journey of rescue, recovery, and transformation. I didn't always recognize it at the time, but I saw it now as I looked back. It started at my hearing when I had to admit that I had a problem that I was incapable of overcoming in my own power. Denial had to be put aside, and I had to face head-on my own defects of character and my broken life. This happened when my pain became greater than my fear of exposure. I was through with fighting, and I was finished with the façade. Even in my twelve-step program I knew that my problem was deeper than alcohol. The alcohol was just a symptom of a deeper evil and destructive addiction that held me captive. While others knew of my alcohol problem, I was pretty good at keeping the underlying beast hidden from the view of everyone. In one way I was thankful that I had been caught at my crime. Secrecy was no longer an option.

However, even though I admitted I had a problem, I had no ability to pry myself free. I prayed until I was blue in the face for over ten years, but nothing changed. I prayed and prayed to have the painful anomaly of my life removed, but it never went away. After praying so hard for so long, I had profound doubts about whether a higher power could really be of any help. Looking back I realized that I was praying to a god of my own understanding. This god was rooted in Mother Earth, or the Spirit of the Universe, but I had little knowledge of the biblical Jesus. I knew nothing of a God who was my Savior.

The grand turning point was that moment in the darkness of my miserable confinement, in the place of my greatest despair, when I came to the end of myself and opened my heart to the love and grace of Jesus. That was when everything changed. I prayed in the name of Jesus, and a new reality took hold of my life. In the past I had spent years in a twelve-step program and read all they had written about sex and lust. I worked the program, made amends, helped others, prayed incessantly, and tried to do all I could to be free. Yet I hit a wall of sheer exhaustion and frustration, and I lost hope that the power higher than myself could restore me to sanity. I was doing my job but, alas! at the end of the line I was still bound in the throes of my unseen and hidden addiction.

But now everything was different. Once I accepted Jesus Christ as my Savior and Lord and began praying in Jesus' name, the tormenting thoughts and drives started going away. It was the first time in my life! I had believed, not in the god of my own understanding but in the God that has revealed himself in Scripture. I believed that he existed, that I was important to him, and that he alone had the power to break the chains of my addiction. At first I was tentative, then over and over again I saw him giving me the strength to overcome my addiction and walk in freedom.

At first it was hard to assess if the freedom was real. After all I was secluded behind locked doors and not fully able to act on my impulses. But the pivotal moment came when I was released to the halfway house. The protective boundaries were gone, and the temptations were square in my path. Could the God who had *set* me free *keep* me free? Overnight I went from incarceration to being slammed with opportunities for lust at every turn. I knew the strength of my addiction, too. It was a hell. My life had been controlled by a strong drive fueled by adrenaline, fear, lust, anxiety, excitement, and dark exhilaration, all charged together, bringing me to a realm so intoxicating that it rivaled any drug. The enemy had a powerful weapon that he had used against me, and I was putty in his hands. But God had intervened, plucked me from the grip of the enemy, and brought me to a new place. I pressed into him and faced the temptations. How would I fare? As I began to encounter the old triggers, I couldn't believe what was happening! The old drives were absent. It was like God had a protective barrier around me. He took away the old heart and the dark urges and gave me a new heart. I kept praying, and I kept working my program—doing the next right thing. But it was different now. The freedom that I had deep within gave me the strength and power to walk in a new way. Each time I was able to resist a temptation to indulge the old addiction, my new resolve fortified within me. I knew I was a walking miracle.

The word "surrender" began to take on new meaning to me. In the past I had tried to surrender and give my will and my life to God, but that god for me had been some nebulous spirit in the sky. I was agnostic in my beliefs and soon become atheistic in my thinking and worldview. At the time I could see no evidence that God was real. But he wouldn't let me stay in that place. He pursued me in love, and I looked up in my pain. I gave up and surrendered to the Jesus of Scripture. Everything was hugely different when I yielded to the care and control of Jesus Christ. When I released my will and life to his will, everything changed. A new me was born.

One of the moments of great release came when I knew I could confess what I had been and what I had done to God. I had walked through most of my life in a place of intense guilt, shame, and remorse.

I hated myself a lot of the time and felt that I was despicable to the core. When I prayed that prayer in prison, I poured out all the baggage and broken pieces of my life to God and felt a strange lightening of my load. He really could handle my stuff.

Now I was finally home. Home with my wife and children. I just wanted to touch their faces and hear their voices. I just wanted to sit and watch them breathe. My journey had been to hell, but I had come through to tell about it. Through the tattered remnants of my life emerged a profound story of the depth and breadth that God would go to rescue one such as me. It demonstrated his huge capacity to save me. The prison doors had been opened, and I had walked free; both the clanking metal door of my incarceration and the dark strangling door of my addiction. God was faithful. The same God who had set me free was showing me that he would keep me free.

"So if the Son sets you free, you will be free indeed." John 8:36

CHAPTER TEN

Awakened by Love

Held in Love

There was a chapter that lay behind me, and yet I sensed that there was a grand and new adventure that waited ahead. I found myself looking forward with anticipation, yet at the same time trying to absorb all the events that had transpired in my life. The final court hearing had taken place, and Matt had gone to prison. It was remarkable to realize that instead of fear and trepidation from the encounter with a deadly knife, I was instead feeling immersed in love. The love I felt was so real, so tangible, so present. Many times after kissing my husband good night I would lie in bed awake and feel cradled in a supernatural embrace. It was as if God was pouring into me exactly what I needed for the healing of my heart. During this time I came to a vivid realization that it was the envelopment of this love that was carrying me, supporting me, nurturing me, empowering me, and breathing new life into me daily.

Scripture came alive. I began to see the great compassion of God woven through every page. God watched over the Israelites as they wandered through a barren wasteland on the way to the land he had promised to give them. As they stood at the entrance to the Promised Land, Moses recounted their journey. The words of this stalwart leader in Deuteronomy carry a poignancy and depth of emotion that can only be imagined. In metaphorical imagery, Moses appeals to the hearts of the people to look back and see how the Lord has cared for them. He passionately reminds, "There you saw how the LORD your God carried you, as a father carries his son, all the way you went until you reached this place."[25] Carried by the Lord. Carried by the love and tenderness of a father for his son. That word picture burned into my mind. It was just how I felt. Carried by the Lord.

Other Scriptures began to come into clearer view and seemed to jump off the page as I read. As I mentioned before there was the favorite one in Ephesians with the great *but*. It is a *but* that changes everything. "*But* because of his great love for us, God, who is rich in mercy . . ."[26] I spent hours contemplating those words. Before the *but* we were dead in sin, following the ruler of the kingdom of the air, gratifying the cravings of our sinful nature and were objects of wrath. Then everything changes! After the *but,* we are alive with Christ, figuratively seated with him in the heavenly realms, immersed in his riches, and saved for eternity. His love changes everything. I knew this was true. My life had been changed, and I knew it was only because of this undeserved love. Sometimes I would just stare up at the sky in gratitude.

Several years after the court hearing, God brought this message of his love home to me in a way I couldn't miss. My husband and three sons and I were on a summer trip to Lake Powell with my extended family, piling eighteen people onto a houseboat and cruising up the serene waterways lined with rugged regal cliffs of sandstone. After the first few days the weather turned sour, and we found ourselves hunkering down on a protected beach, trying to keep our personal items from being carried away by the gusts of wind. At one point we watched as our queen size air mattress lifted off the top of the boat and tumbled end over end clear across the bay, carried by an unusually strong gale. However, instead of the storm passing after a few days, it continued throughout the week. By the weekend, we had a case of cabin fever that needed severe attention. Of the eighteen people on board, ten were children, and they were ready to expend some serious pent up energy.

On Saturday morning we noticed that the lake was still too turbulent for skiing or water play, but the hills behind us were open for discovery. The skies had cleared even though a steady breeze continued to blow. We gathered the children in the cabin of the boat and came up with a plan. We would go in search of things that spoke to us of God. At the end of the day, we would gather again in the boat, and each one would share their find. After a short pep talk and prayer for God to reveal himself to us through the desert wonders around us, we set out on our adventure. Some of us headed down the beach. Others climbed the sandstone ridge. Others peeked and poked through the bushes lining the water's edge. A couple of the older boys lit firecrackers on top of some rocks for good measure. All in all, it turned out to be a beautiful day, and eighteen people gathered together in the living area of the boat after sundown to share the treasures in their pockets and buckets.

As we shared stories and sightings, we reveled together at the glory and majesty of God. He truly had created an extraordinary place for us to live. Hidden in the cracks and recesses of the earth were his treasures, waiting for discovery, and we all had a sense that he was taking great delight in our enthusiasm. After the last rock collection had been shared and the final story had been told, I found myself ready to retire and enjoy the quiet of the night. With these images and thoughts running through my mind, I climbed the steps to the top of the boat where we laid out our sleeping bags each night. Far from the lights of any city, the storm had now cleared and the sky was a solid sea of stars. Laying down on one of the bags, I gazed up at the blanket of stars overhead and again marveled at the vastness of their expanse and the God who held it all together.

All of a sudden I noticed a constellation that just seemed to leap from the sky. It formed a perfect heart, right side up, and directly over my head. A smile broke out on my face, and I uttered the words that just seemed natural for the moment, "God, is that for me?" No sooner did the words leave my mouth than a shooting star burst through the center of the heart like an arrow from Cupid's bow. I couldn't believe it! Did I just see that? Tears began streaming down my cheeks. He loved me. He had spoken his love, written in the sky. How could he have that kind of love for me, inadequate and flawed as I am? Who is this God that loves with such depth and magnitude? My initial instinct was to feel unworthy of the love and retreat into a place of hiding. Yet something drew me out of myself and into his warm embrace that night. That evening I knew it was a message that God intended me to know, to absorb, and to treasure. In that moment of epiphany, I knew I was embarking on a journey where he would teach me more about how to receive his incredible love, how to absorb its healing power, how to open my heart, and how to let him access all the hidden fears and barricaded insecurities that lay within. It was a moment that would change my life for the years to come. I knew the message of his love was to be central to my life. Tears again fell freely from my eyes as I stared up at the universe and knew God had spoken. It was his message, and he wanted it broadcast far and wide, one for everyone to hear.

Every year we returned to this lake in Arizona, I would look for the heart in the sky again. Time after time I would see it shining in the sea of stars and find myself reminded of the night when his great love broke through in a new way. Later I learned that the right flank of the star heart was formed by a constellation named "Corona Borealis," Latin for "Northern Crown." The seven stars that make up this constellation were given their name in the days of Greek mythology, inspired by the semi-circular shape of a crown. This group of stars now has deep meaning for me. How fitting that God should express his love through a constellation named for a crown. To me, it was the crown of thorns that Jesus wore when he hung from a Roman cross two thousand years ago, demonstrating the greatest love that mankind will ever see. The cross—the ultimate picture of perfect love.

As time went by I found myself trying to understand this kind of love. It was truly the source of my healing and the strength of my life. Even though I didn't fully understand it, I found myself just resting in it. Soon I realized that the love I was experiencing from God was changing how I saw myself. A new security was taking root in the depths of my heart. A new freedom was emerging to be my true self. I felt loved and treasured, and the depth to which these emotions sank into my life astounded me. His love was real! The more I opened my heart to it, the more it just seemed to push out the false perceptions I carried, the hurts that I harbored, and the insecurities that I bore.

But the story of redemption didn't end there. Jesus Christ was raised on the third day and ascended to the heavens where he now sits at the right hand of God the Father. I saw that now another crown is worn—not a crown with thorns digging into his brow, but the crown of a king. No longer a battered and bruised body, but a victorious and powerful Lord. The crown of a king is worn, reminding us that he is worthy of being exalted, worshipped, and adored by those he has saved. He is a king of love, and his love changes everything. No wonder he chose the Northern Crown to make his heart in the sky.

In the seventeenth century, a Scottish minister named Henry Scougal wrote a book entitled, *The Life of God in the Soul of Man*. His book was intended as a letter to a friend but was later found and published because of its insight into the love of God. One quote in particular has found its way into the modern era with renewed impact.

> *"The worth and excellency of a soul is to be measured*
> *by the object of its love; he who loveth mean and sordid*
> *things, doth thereby become base and vile; but a noble*
> *and well placed affection doth advance and improve*
> *the Spirit into a conformity with the perfections which*
> *it loves."*[27]

I had come face to face with the love of God. First, through an encounter with a dangerous assailant after which I realized that even in the midst of that dreadful moment I was being held. Second, in that moment far from home when God had broadcast his love in a life-changing display in the sky. I realized that his love was present every moment of every day, and that I was never outside of that love. The more I allowed his love to permeate my being, the more I found my own heart being challenged. He was truly doing his work of conforming me to be more like himself.

Risk to Love

Learning to open my heart to the love of God and offering my own imperfect attempts of love back to him has been a journey of discovery. It became clear that love is a risk. In order to love, one must open up the heart and become vulnerable—vulnerable to rejection or dismissal. For those burned by human love this can sometimes be a difficult thing. Yet, I found the more God revealed himself to me, the more I knew I could trust him fully with my heart. I could receive his unconditional love and rest in the unfaltering acceptance that was there for me. But it was also a risk to give it back. Somewhere deep inside I realized this relationship with Jesus had to go both ways, yet my own love seemed so inadequate, so small compared to his.

The biblical Mary, sister of Martha and Lazarus, became a heroine in my eyes. While Matthew and Mark tell her story, the book of John[28] gives more context to her actions. Mary had just seen Jesus perform one of his greatest miracles when he raised her brother Lazarus from the dead after being in the tomb for four days. She had stood near her Lord as he had shed tears, sympathizing with the deep grief of those he loved. She heard his prayer to his Father and then probably uttered a gasp as she saw her shrouded brother emerge from the dark cavern that had held captive his decaying body. Mary, who had once sat at the feet of Jesus, learned from his teaching, witnessed his power, and now desired to respond to his love.

At great risk she showed up with a courageous plan at a dinner given in Jesus' honor. As he sat reclining at the table she slipped up to his side, carefully removed the costly perfume from her cloak, and, without shrinking back, proceeded to empty its contents on his gravel-dusted feet. Without succumbing to the disapproving looks of those around her, she continued in her act of devotion. Pulling the pin from her hair she allowed the long tresses to fall, cascading over her master's feet. At this point she may have been so caught up in her display of adoration that she tuned all others out and allowed her love to flow uninhibited. What a risk! Would he mock her? Would he ignore her? Would he be ashamed of her and push her away?

As I focused on this scriptural portrait I began to realize that others had taken the risk. Some had been willing to open up their hearts to deep love and others had offered their own in return without thought to the consequences. Mary's love was accepted, treasured, and valued by Jesus. Her act of devotion won his heart. Her story would be told around the globe. It was clear that God was inviting me to that same place with him.

Invitation to Pursuit

Some years later God used another story to teach me even deeper lessons of his love. He had written his own heart's passion in the sky; he had drawn me to himself; he had quenched my fears so that I was willing to take the risk to love him back, and now he was taking me to yet another new place: teaching me to pursue him.

My oldest son who was thirteen at the time of the attack was now a handsome man of twenty-two and interested in a beautiful young lady he had secretly admired at school for some time. She was vivacious and full of life, and they had just had a whirlwind of a summer, filled with fun and together time. In just a few days she would be leaving for New Zealand for a nine-month stay with a youth program, and my son would be returning to college for his senior year. They had both discovered feelings for each other at the beginning of the summer and had spent almost every day checking activities off their dream "to do" list. The dream list included all kinds of random activities from cooking sushi, to white water rafting, to sitting on top of a hill and watching the sunrise. They had created their list at the beginning of the summer in a mood of adventure and delight with life, and now, as the summer ended, they realized that almost everything on the list had been accomplished. What a summer it had been! How to celebrate a great three months of a newly found love and friendship and make a memory to carry through the long stretch ahead? My son, Brent, thought a treasure hunt would be a perfect ending to their summer together.

It began with an invitation to Erica to come over for dinner at Brent's house. She was to arrive at half past five, but when she knocked on the door, to her surprise she found no one home. Some mistake had been made! It was then that she noticed a note on the door that told her to call him on his cell phone. The voice on the other end of the line directed her down to the tree-lined pond a distance behind the house. From there, the clues led her to a myriad of places that held fond, summer memories for both of them.

At her last stop she found another envelope with a new twist. There were seven dollars with the message, "Here is your entrance fee. Come up to Horsetooth Lake and walk down to the dock. You will find something there."

Erica arrived in the park near the lake and walked down to the dock. There she found Brent waiting in his father's boat to take her for an evening cruise around the lake. But that was not all. A full meal had been prepared and was spread out on a tablecloth: fettuccini and salad, bread, and tiramisu. There were candles lit for the occasion, and his guitar. Brent had even written her a song for the occasion. What a spectacular evening! What a friendship to celebrate!

Erica, being the ever thoughtful and gracious young woman that she is, chose to say "thank you" with a book of her own creation. It was a remembrance book of the summer that the two had shared together. She recounted the journeys and the adventures, the laughter and the delight, the moments of surprise and the tenderness of new love. Every page started with a new letter of the alphabet as she used pictures and verse, artistry and creativity to highlight their treasured moments.

I will never forget their treasure hunt because of the words written in the book she gave my son. She wrote, "Brent, you made a treasure hunt for me, and I found you!" For Erica, the treasure at the end of the hunt was the person who was waiting to be found. Erica could have written, "You made me a great dinner," or "You wrote me a beautiful song," or even "You surprised me like I've never been surprised before." But even though those things might have been true and a part of the story, she focused on the heart of the hunt. The one who was pursuing her and wooing her had been found, and that was the delight and joy to be celebrated.

As I think back on the "treasure hunt" of love that God has brought me on, I have tears of joy in my eyes. God has created quite a treasure hunt for us. It must delight him to think of the things he has prepared for us, and he must long for desire to be awakened in us and cause us to go searching for him. He doesn't hide because he wants to stay distant. The truth is, he is pursuing and wooing us. He hides at times because he wants to be found, and his joy is great when we embark on the journey of discovery. He must love sending clues along the way to entice us onward toward him. He knows that the greatest treasure is himself. He is a treasure that satisfies all our longings.

As God has taught me more about his love, a Scripture in Jeremiah came to life. "'You will seek me and find me when you seek me with all your heart. I will be found by you,' declares the LORD."[29] The great "I AM," the Lord of the heavens, the king of creation, the ruler of the universe, the Holy One who keeps all things by the breath of his mouth, allows himself to be found. And you can say of him as Erica did years ago, "You made a treasure hunt for me, and I found you!"

In the days, months, and years following the traumatic events of the assault, there have been countless challenges and difficulties, and life has thrown numerous curve balls in my direction. Yet, something was implanted deep within my heart that has remained unshakable and firm. It is this truth: He is my greatest treasure. The love of God through Jesus Christ, and what he did to demonstrate that love by dying on a cross, has transformed my life. He has awakened my heart to love, to healing, to belonging, and to new life.

Paul says in Philippians, "What is more, I consider everything a loss because of the surpassing worth of knowing Christ Jesus my Lord, for whose sake I have lost all things. I consider them garbage, that I may gain Christ and be found in him."[30] Nothing else compares. Nothing else will bring abundant life. Thank God that he allows himself to be found. And what a supply of delights he has waiting—security and belonging, peace and rest, light and renewal. Praise God for the treasure of him.

Brent and Erica had been married just two months when we returned again as a family to Lake Powell. One evening, my new daughter-in-law and I climbed the steps to the top of the boat, taking a quiet moment to catch up and visit about the day. The rest of the family was laughing and enjoying games below us as we lay on our backs and gazed into a dark and overcast sky. There were no stars out that night due to a dense cloud cover, but I began to tell her of the heart in the sky and how we had looked for it every year since it had first been spotted. It was such a regular reminder of God's great love. As we spoke together looking at the cloudy sky above, suddenly something happened that literally took our breath away. Neither of us could even speak. I pointed upward unable to form words, barely able to produce a motion. We both gazed in awe as we watched the thick clouds open up a hole in the sky. The only stars in the entire heavens that we could see came shining through that hole. They were the stars of the heart. For just a few moments the clouds framed the heart and then slowly drifted back into place, obscuring the stars we had just seen. The sky returned to blackness, but we cried out in amazement: "Did you see that?" "Wow, that was just incredible!" Our heavenly Father had again spoken his love, and we were overwhelmed. How could we ever doubt? He had written it in the sky.

As the years have gone on I have found myself contemplating such a vast and abundant love. It occurred to me that love, rather than humility, is the antithesis of pride. Pride is turning inward, being self-consumed, often leading to narcissism. But love is the epitome of outward expression. It focuses on the one loved, takes great delight in the other, and longs to see goodness poured into the lives of those outside itself. The ultimate love the world has ever known is the love of God that gave everything to rescue, restore, and renew.

God had a work to do in me and still does. He is teaching me that love is a two-way relationship. He is giving me the ability to love him more deeply and to hear more clearly when he speaks. He is opening my ears to listen and to be sensitive to the promptings of his Spirit. He is teaching me how to posture myself so I can live fully engaged in this dynamic relationship. In the love of God, my life has found a depth of security and serenity that is surprising yet real. It gives me the confidence to step out and be all that I am created to be. It provides the freedom to love him and others more fully. I know who is holding me, who will always be faithful, and whose love will never fail. It is a place he is inviting us all to live.

He desires every day to ground our hearts deeper into the truths of Paul's words in Romans, "For I am convinced that neither death nor life, neither angels nor demons, neither the present nor the future, nor any powers, neither height nor depth, nor anything else in all creation, will be able to separate us from the love of God that is in Christ Jesus our Lord."[31]

CHAPTER ELEVEN

Path of Healing

Is It Real?

Home. Could it be true? Was I home for good? I found myself looking at my watch over and over. Deep down I wondered when the time would be up and I would have to return to my cold, bleak apartment. I had been on a rigid schedule for so long. Then I was jarred by reality. It was like suddenly waking up from an ugly nightmare and realizing that what I was seeing right then was truly real. Yes, I was home to stay. I couldn't believe I was there.

It seemed like I had been gone for twenty years. So much had changed. I had been allowed to come home on a trial run over the weekend just a few months earlier. It was the first time I had seen my home in five years. At that time I was shocked when our family Rottweiler, Sarah, came running up to me to sniff out this stranger in the house. She was big and fat! Amazement tangled with shock and disbelief felt in the pit of my stomach. "What happened to you?" I stammered. Glancing around the room, everything looked foreign. I didn't recognize much from that day long ago when I said good-bye to my family and left for the court hearing. Over the five years that I was away my wife had accumulated a lot of things. No, she didn't buy new furniture. But a myriad of trinkets and knickknacks covered most of the surfaces of the room. A deep remorse suddenly took hold of my heart. It all seemed so symbolic. In that moment, it was as if I could see a little snapshot into my wife's heart. She had been searching for some kind of security, some kind of comfort in the midst of the chaos I had brought into her life. A wave of realization hit me hard. I did this. All that I could see was a direct result of what I've done.

The sound of my son's voice brought me out of my momentary reflection. I could get swept away by the tidal wave of regret if I wasn't careful. Better to remember how far I had come rather than grieve over where I had been. Regret could consume me and be a sure path to self-destruction. I was being given a second chance, and I was determined to put everything I had into it.

Over the next few days, I marveled at the things around me like someone seeing the ocean for the first time. So much to experience. So much to absorb. We ordered Papa Murphy's pizza, and I sunk my teeth into the thick soft cheese in pure enjoyment. The chain had come to Colorado during my incarceration, so this was new—a pizza you could pick up already made and bake at home. I was on cloud nine. Food had been pretty hard to stomach in the halfway house and my own cooking in the apartment wasn't much better. I had lived on sandwiches for a year. Now I could sit down and have pizza with my wife and kids. I even got a real stainless steel fork to eat it with. Life just couldn't get much better.

So many times I had been here in my dreams. It was what kept me going for all those years. I still had to pinch myself that I was really looking into the eyes of the most beautiful woman I had ever seen—my wife. There had been so much loss in prison, and there were days that I didn't know how I was going to make it. The remorse had been great, and the realization of all I would never get back was more than I could bear. Much of the time the only hope I clung to was my wife.

How could she have stayed with me? How did she survive what I put her through? She believed in me when I didn't even believe in myself. She looked like an angel standing in front of me.

Oh, but there were rough spots for her. After I came home I found out that a few years into my incarceration she had doubted whether she could be with me. Unbeknownst to me, she was struggling with our relationship and entertaining thoughts of leaving. She got to the point where she was talking herself out of staying with me and beginning to think about past boyfriends. She just didn't want to tell me while in prison, worried about what I might do. I knew something was up when the phone calls lessened, and there was distance in her voice. But something changed for her, too, when she received Christ into her life. God's grace infused into a painful and difficult relationship, and she hung in there with me. I thank God to this day that I didn't lose her. I know he would have given me the strength to go on had I come home to an empty house, but I am so grateful that I didn't have that loss to face.

Hole in My Heart

There was, however, another loss that I *did* have to face. There was someone who wasn't there to greet me when I returned home. I thought back to a traumatic time, three years into my sentence when I got the strange message. I was in Cell House 9, and so much in my life was soon to unexpectedly change again. My cellmate and I were whittling some time away after work, confined to our living quarters in the closed-security prison facility where we weren't allowed to walk around. A guard who was normally quite friendly, even to us inmates, approached me with a solemn look on his face. Without explanation he handed me a pass to the chaplain's office. "What is this?" I thought. "I don't go to church here."

My cellmate, who had been in prison for sixteen years at the time, shook his head and looked at me with a strange fear on his face. "I can tell you it's usually not good when you get those passes." The fear on his face transferred to mine and my gut seized up within me. Someone had clearly died. But who could it be? My family was very small so there weren't too many options. I had just spoken with my wife and knew that she and the kids were okay. My mom, my dad, and my sister were all healthy. There was nothing wrong with any of them. Quickly I took the pass and headed out the door, knowing there was bad news waiting for me yet unable to imagine what it could be.

The chaplain was also solemn. "I regret to inform you that your father has passed away." My dad? Surely he wasn't talking about my stepdad who had adopted me and raised me since I was nine months old. He was only fifty-six years old and had just received a clean bill of health from his doctor. My stepdad was a college swimmer, not over-weight, and had just had a complete physical, coming through with flying colors. No, the chaplain must be talking about my biological father, a man that I had never met. I waited. Then I asked again, "My dad?" "Yes," was his reply, "Robert." I went numb. It was my stepdad, the man who had been a father to me my entire life.

Finally I uttered a few words through my whitened lips. "Wow, what happened?" The chaplain looked back at me with sadness, shook his head, and said, "I don't know that. I just need to inform you that he has passed away." It was such a quick conversation, but the blow to my being was profound. I'm not sure how my feet found their way without a brain to direct them, but somehow I ended up back at the cell house looking into the face of my cellmate who was anticipating my return. In a dazed, shocked voice I choked out the news, "My dad died," then blankly looked around the room as if there were some answers mysteriously transcribed on the wall to explain it all. Focusing again on my cellmate, I blurted out the words with all the emotion building up in me, "My dad died!" In a moment of empathy my cellmate reached out and held my hands. He spoke no words, but I knew he was there for me. He could see my pain. I knew he cared.

Just looking into the eyes of someone who was concerned was all it took. The floodgates opened, and I burst into sobs. My stepdad was the man I had looked up to more than any other in the world. He was the only male figure in my life, and he had been there for me. I remembered when he had taken the time to drive my wife and children the several hour trip to the prison so they could visit me. He had done that twice. My dad knew it was important to me and important to them, and he wanted to make it happen. He was my rock, and now he was gone. It just didn't seem real.

With a broken heart I left to find some of my other friends to share what had happened. One suggested, "You should see if you can go to the funeral." I knew that was never going to happen. But my friend insisted, "No, they try to accommodate inmates who have lost a family member." Since he knew a lot more about the prison system than I did, I decided to take a chance.

One of the guards helped me put together a request for the prison warden. From what I could tell, it would take an act of God for me to be released to go. Well, I found out God is still doing acts. My request was granted. Three days later, two armed guards picked me up in the morning, shackled me real good, loaded me on to the Department of Corrections van, and drove me five hours to the Kibbey-Fishburn Funeral Home in Loveland, Colorado. I was in full prison greens with my hands cuffed and ankles shackled. In addition to this I had a chain around my waist to which my handcuffs were attached and then another chain from my waist down to the leg shackles. I clinked and rattled whenever I moved and felt like the rusty Tin Man of Oz.

Pulling into my hometown was more overwhelming than I had expected. Loveland had been my home since I was four years old, yet coming back to it inundated me with a barrage of stimuli. At this point I hadn't been outside of prison for three and a half years. I hadn't seen vehicles or people with clothes on for a very long time. Well, clothes that weren't green, that is. A host of emotions fueled the overload in my mind.

As soon as we pulled up to the funeral home, the guard next to me pulled out a knife and, brandishing it in a brazen display, said, "If you try to run . . ." As he shook the knife in my face, his meaning was clear. However, the knife was the least of my concerns. I had no intention of running. If I had wanted to run, I could have jumped out of the window in the courtroom long ago and saved myself a lot of prison-time anguish . . . well, maybe. No, I knew I wasn't going to run. There was something else, though, that consumed me with fear. It was the hundreds of cars in the parking lot. I knew they belonged to a multitude of family friends, those who had known my father for years. He was an electrical engineer with Hewlett-Packard and well respected in the community, having lived in Loveland for most of his life. How could I possibly face all these people? Looking like this? It was enough to make all my courage evaporate. Then I received more startling news.

The driver informed us that the funeral had been detained for almost an hour waiting for me to arrive! There was no backing out now. I was sure that changing my mind was not an option, and the guards on either side would make sure that I made their trip north worthwhile. They would force me to go whether I wanted to or not. I felt panic and shame mixed with dread. Then it came to me. I am going to do this. I have to do this!

The back door to the chapel swung open, and I stood there, wearing full greens, chains wrapped around every extremity, and flanked by my armed guards. Every eye was on me. There was a packed house, and now the wayward, iniquitous son had arrived. At first I just hung my head in overt shame, feeling I was disgracing my family and shocking their friends. At that moment an uncanny freedom and peace poured over me that is hard to explain. I had nothing left to hide. All my failure was out in the open for all to see. Some of my parent's friends knew of my situation, and others did not. For those who didn't know, they knew now. Hopefully they could figure out what they were seeing. In a strange way it brought comfort to my humiliated heart. I realized, "I just don't care. I really don't care what anyone thinks. I'm here for my dad. I'm here because I want to honor the man who meant so much to me."

We started to walk up the center aisle as my heavy chains clanked and clattered with each small and halting step. The shuffling journey didn't end until we had reached the front row. The two armed sentinels and I found our place next to my wife and children after a brief stop to hug my mom and sister on the other side of the aisle. My mom managed to emit a few words, and they meant a lot to me, "I love you, honey. I'm so glad you could be here." I knew I had become the center of attention, so I was relieved when the service started and we could focus on Dad.

Most of us were in shock with his death. He was so young. A number was posted on a board in front of the chapel. It was the number of his days walking the earth: 20,440. Is that all? Is that all the days he had? Why have I wasted so many of them in my own life? The blunt force of time and its limitations hit me hard. What am I doing with my cache of moments? My dad had made his count. Suddenly the resonating tenor of the pastor's voice shattered my musings. This was about my dad, and they were telling his story.

My father had been helping my brother-in-law put in a sandbox in the backyard for his son. It was a clear, cool day, about noon, when my dad began complaining that he was feeling hot and thirsty. This caused some alarm since it wasn't that warm outside. He came inside, poured himself a glass of water, and plunked down on the couch. Something didn't seem right, so my sister's husband called an ambulance. Dad was not the least concerned and even joked about the perceived overreaction of his son-in-law. When the paramedics came, my dad chastised them a bit for their zealousness in checking him out, insisting that he was okay. "This is stupid!" he protested, but they insisted. "We're just going to check you out. It's precautionary." On the ride to the hospital my dad continued in his dispute in his usual light-hearted manner, "What, do you think I am going to die on the way to the hospital or something?" And he did. A massive coronary. He had never had any heart problems, and his clean bill of health had been given just three days earlier. There was no time for my family to prepare. We were still reeling.

The pastor continued, then opened up the question, "Does anyone want to come up to share a memory?" Immediately I felt all the eyes of my family on me. I drew from the scant well of courage deep inside of me and thought, "I'm here. And I'm here for a reason. I may not even understand now, but I need to do this." I wasn't prepared and didn't even know what I was going to say, but I rose to my feet, flanked by my weapon-clad friends, and clattered my way to the podium. At this point I was fully exposed so there was nothing to lose. The words began to flow.

Without trembling or fear I spoke, "I apologize and regret that I am standing here like this today. Robert is my father, and I want to say a couple of things about what kind of man he was." I began to describe his great sense of humor and recalled important memories of times I had spent with this man who was both my hero and my friend. One of my most profound recollections was playing Pictionary with him. I recounted how he would get tongue tied like the time I drew a snowstorm. In his enthusiasm and thrill at figuring it out he yelled, "Snorm! . . . Snorm! . . . Snow Snorm! . . . Snow Snorm!" I responded,

"You're close, Dad, but . . ." At this I heard laughter throughout the chapel, and my heart swelled with pride that I could play a part in memorializing a man who had impacted me so much.

The moments after I spoke were just a fleeting blur. The funeral was over, I quickly said good-bye to my family and was whisked away to the van. Well, the "whisking" might be a bit of an exaggeration. I didn't move too fast in my body armor of chains. Soon we were back on the road to prison. But something had changed inside of me through the experience. My heart felt a new freedom. An unexpected elation broke through the dark walls of shame and remorse that I had erected. I was so glad I was there. It felt good to be doing something that built up rather than tore down. The man I was becoming took another step in the direction of wholeness that day. I had been in a battle with fear and shame that day, and these enemies had wielded ugly weapons and intimidating tactics. Yet I had persevered, pressed through, and overcome them for that moment. It occurred to me that it was God who had given me the strength to do it. I was still new to his love and provision, but he had come through. I thought about these things all the way back to jail.

Now, here I was at home, two years after that profound day. The regret again began to seep through the cracks and crevices of my reminiscences. He couldn't see me now. My dad couldn't see how I had changed and how things had worked out. When he had died I felt that a part of me had died too. There was a big hollow hole inside. I thought I was as hollow as I could get when in prison, but I found the hollowness could still increase. What would I do with this cavity that regret wanted to fill? That day, as I looked around my home, knowing I had been given a new start and a new chance, I knew I was going to do everything possible to live my life in a way that mattered. I was going to do it for my dad, for myself, for God. I was going to make my short days on earth the best they could be. I was going to make my mom, my wife, and my children proud of me. With God's help, I was going to live out the new man that I knew God had recreated on the inside.

Settling In

Choices. I knew I had choices to make. God had broken me free, and he had brought me on the long journey to home. He had done something for me that I couldn't have done for myself. He had shattered the hold of my addiction and opened the door to the prison that had kept me bound up for so long. For a moment I allowed myself to think back on that time. The addiction was insidious, and I never knew it had taken hold until I was confined in its strangling grip. It was debilitating, crippling, and truly more of a prison than the physical one I finally entered. I was chained to that thing, that beast, that driving lust. All those years that I was in a twelve-step program, I knew I wasn't an alcoholic. I did drink too much for sure, but it wasn't the underlying problem. Drinking and drugs were just a symptom of a much bigger issue. It wasn't too difficult to quit drinking, but the bigger problem never quit. Beneath the surface it lurked and stealthily hid, waiting for an opportune moment to erupt and show its ugly head.

Soaking up the warmth of my home and glancing at the faces of my wife and children, who were now studying me with intrigue, brought me back to the current reality. I never wanted to go back to that place again. I would voluntarily submit to the changes that God wanted to keep making in my life. I would trust him to continue in his work of transformation. I would lay down my naturally independent spirit and keep trusting in him to shape my character.

A few days later, I had another first. I got my driver's license! It had been so long since I had been behind the wheel of a car. I was granted a new freedom. It wasn't long before we were able to purchase a second car, and a whole new world opened up. Life was moving forward. Since I was still on parole, and would be for another four years, I continued in the routine of all my treatment programs. I went to two-hour group sessions with my therapist every Wednesday night, met with my parole officer every two weeks, and took a polygraph test every three months. In addition to that, my wife and I attended a couples group every Friday night. These were meetings with other offenders who were trying to integrate back into life with their wives and families.

The treatment schedule had begun in the halfway house and continued for six years. I was required to pay for all of it, including every polygraph test and all other evaluative tests. Overall I figured that it cost me about fifty thousand dollars. But I had no complaint. It was what I had to do. I don't regret one dollar that I had to spend. I was home. Throughout those years, I think I learned every technique and psychological theory out there to help those like me. It was hoped that if I were exposed to enough cognitive behavioral restructuring and covert desensitization tools, my deviant actions would be corrected. If I learned enough techniques for monitoring bad behavior, they thought I would be well adjusted and able to be an upstanding citizen. If I could pass a plethora of polygraph tests, it was assumed that I was honest and rehabilitated. While there is value in all those things, deep down I knew the truth. Unless God had intervened in my life and changed my heart at its core, none of those things would have worked. I would have been no more than a painted tomb, able to comply and look okay on the outside, but still dead, dark, and driven on the inside. Only God could change me where it really counted.

As the days and years moved forward in my new life at home, I tried to stay in a place of cooperation with God's plan. I learned to focus on the good things and to remember the long way that God had brought me. All the effort and hardship I had gone through started becoming more and more a memory of the past, and I chose not to dwell on it. I could have gotten bogged down in it because the loss was great. The time seemed to move so slowly in prison and sometimes the discouragement, depression, guilt, shame, and remorse were unbearable. When I allowed myself to think about it, I became painfully aware that a big chunk of my life was gone. Every twenty-four hours away from my kids had been pure agony knowing they were without a dad another day. I knew I could never get those years back.

However, something surprising was happening here at home. With each passing day back at home, the pain and regret of the memories lifted a little more, and I seemed just a little further removed from my ordeal. It wasn't long before the loss seemed smaller and smaller and finally was gone. My perspective changed. I didn't lose anything. I gained everything. What needed to happen, happened. I needed to go to prison for God to break into my heart. I needed all that time. I needed to experience the pit to appreciate the sunlight. My life wasn't wasted. God was using it all. My life needed to be completely torn down to the basement level, and the foundation had to be rebuilt. Now my foundation was Jesus Christ. If this is what it took to pluck me out of the hell I had been in, then I am forever grateful. There is no insincerity when I say that I wouldn't trade a day of it because I know what my life is like today. I wouldn't trade one of these days for a hundred of the days before.

In 2005, I was finally off parole. My parole officer felt I had received everything I could get out of treatment and group sessions, so that season came to a close too. It had been a long journey. I had been under supervision with daily monitoring for nine and a half years. It was pretty uneventful since I was well grounded in my new life. My routine was predictable. I went to work and then straight home and stayed there. I just wanted to be home.

As the years rolled on, the relationship with my wife and children grew stronger. I poured myself into my family and worked hard to provide for them. I was proud of my work and knew that I was doing the best with my hands as a woodworker and being the best husband and father that I could be. The rewards soon followed. My children expressed love. They told me they thought I was cool. They rearranged their schedules to hang out with me. I was the dad they needed.

My relationship with my wife was also better than it ever was. I thought back to the day I came home on a trial visit after being gone for nearly five years. I got to sleep in my own bed with my wife. It was monumental. God continued to connect us more and more emotionally and spiritually. I love her more today than ever before, and I know she loves me. This alone is a miracle.

Nagging Guilt

There was much that was good, yet there were still significant challenges. While I had experienced the radical forgiveness of God while in prison, there was another component to forgiveness I struggled with for some time—forgiving myself. I had hurt my family so badly and had wounded others around me. I had traumatized my victim and knew I had caused pain to her and her family. God had forgiven me; I had received words of forgiveness from others around me, but I still felt stuck. How could I get past the all-consuming remorse that I carried around with me day after day? It was like a pit in my stomach and haunted me from deep within, always taunting me, driving me, and drawing me under with its steely tentacles. I was past the driving force of my addiction, but in another, more subtle way the unresolved self-loathing that lay buried beneath the exterior of recovery was driving me too. I wasn't sure how to deal with it, so I didn't.

All the years in AA had taught me some valuable lessons. I knew that my healing depended on forgiving those who had wronged me and in making amends to those I had wounded. I knew that resentment was the number one offender in those who struggled with addiction. But I knew I wasn't resentful, and I also knew that I had no one around me I needed to forgive. The truth was, the person I was really upset with was me. Not only had I put others through torture, I had put myself through a good dose as well.

So for the next few years I just did what I knew to do. I could be disciplined. And it gave me a measure of relief. The more I did the next right thing, the better I felt about who I was. Every time I said "No!" to the temptations around me, the stronger became my conviction and the deeper became my resolve to be the man I knew God wanted me to be. I went wholeheartedly on, one hundred percent, full steam ahead, trying to do my best in my work, in my relationships, and in my family. It made me feel better about myself, and I could walk with my head up, without feeling ashamed. I learned how to like myself again. The more I made right choices and good, sound decisions, the more I could look at myself as someone to have empathy on. I gave myself some space. I had been a hurting unit, broken and without hope. I didn't know another way to live, and I couldn't see any other options when I had wreaked so much havoc in my life and in the lives of others.

And yet, there was something missing. The deep guilt that remained under the spit-shined exterior. When I had accepted Christ in prison, I was overcome with a sense of freedom and joy. He had broken me loose and forgiven me from the sin in my life. It was glorious. It was life altering. But over the years something had crept into my life. My past had come seeping in, and the guilt had slowly and steadily returned like the rising tide, flooding again the places it had once been. I was home and free, but something deep inside had yet to be released. I knew that God wasn't mad at me, and intellectually I knew that he loved me, and I counted myself as a solid Christian. I went to church periodically and read Scripture here and there. I guess

I felt this was the best it was going to get. If I could just keep myself stable, I would be fine. Life had become routine, and I quite easily settled into the rut of everyday existence. The years rolled by and I kept steady on.

Startling Turn of Events

There was one other thing, however, that continued to plague me. I knew the guilt deep down had to do with my victim. I was afraid I had destroyed her life. The last time I had any contact with Rose was fifteen years ago in the courtroom just before I was handcuffed and led away. I knew getting in touch with her just wouldn't be right. I had traumatized her enough by what I had done. There was really no way of ever having closure with her. Down deep I worried that she might be incapacitated with fear since I had been released from prison. Maybe she thought I was out plotting against her or conniving some way to reenter her life. I would give anything if she could just know how much I had changed, what God had done in breaking me free, and how my life was on a good track now—if I could just tell her. Even if she yelled at me, it would be okay. At least she would know.

I remembered back when I was at the halfway house. My wife and I were allowed to go out for a couple of hours, and she was driving. We were in the parking lot of Lowes, and I saw a car slowly coming in our direction. I recognized that car; it was the one I knew Rose and her husband drove. They were coming toward us and were passing right by our vehicle. Instantly, fear gripped my heart with a power that is hard to describe. I briefly looked up to see their faces. My insides felt like they were going to explode. It wasn't so much a fear for me, but a fear that she had seen me and panicked. I just knew I was the cause of great turmoil in her life. If only I could make it right. If only I could set her free—set us both free.

Many times over the years, because of my work, I had to drive up the main road by her house. I would try to avoid it whenever possible. I just didn't want to see her and add to her pain. When I was forced to take that route I had a sick and dismal feeling take over my gut. It was like I was returning to a morbid and ugly place where I had tried to end my life and possibly hers. I figured this was just a burden I needed to bear. I would keep trying to stay clear of where she might be. Somehow I would deal with the gnawing guilt inside. Maybe I could give it to God and he would know what to do. I began to pray. I prayed specifically. "God, I need you to help me with this. I need you."

Almost ten years had passed since I had returned home. I was comfortable, situated, and content. Other than the latent guilt that I had managed to suppress somewhat, I was doing fine. Life was unremarkable and I liked it that way. My wife looked more and more beautiful to me every day. I liked that too. That is why I immediately perked up when she walked in the door from work with a look on her face that was hard to read. Her news was startling and jarred me to my feet. "I ran into Rose today. She wants to meet with you."

CHAPTER TWELVE

A New Direction

Evil Turned into Good

Years have gone by since the day Matt entered my life. It was the turning point for so much that has transpired since then. When I look back I stand incredulous as I see how the entire trajectory I was on was altered. Remarkably I can view it all today and truthfully say that I wouldn't change a thing. Each trauma and every difficulty seems now to have had a purpose, and the fruit that has come out of it makes every step worth it. Oh, I realize the journey continues and there is never a place of arriving until I draw my last breath, but the journey has become richer, fuller, and more dynamic since the day when life almost came to a halt.

My role as pastor was challenging to say the least. I learned a lot. I struggled with how to tackle such a great task. However, God was teaching me daily how to depend on him. When I was called on to speak, he gave the words. When I had to perform a funeral, he gave the strength and ability to minister to the family. When I officiated a wedding, he poured out great joy and gave the wisdom to counsel and guide. The door opened to be involved with many ministries, including global missions and local outreach, creating a passion deep within for those less fortunate in our world. God placed me in an extraordinary team of other pastors who taught me much. He surrounded me with a talented group of men who believed in the gifts that God gave to women. They encouraged, inspired, and empowered. I am who I am today because of their faithful guidance, loving counsel, and wise mentoring.

After twelve years serving as a pastor, however, I knew that God was calling me to complete my seminary degree. I had begun a Master of Theology degree eight years earlier and was given a ten-year window to finish or lose what I had begun. So in spite of my great love for the pastoral team, staff, and congregation of the church I was serving, I stepped down from the role and started attending school full time at Fuller Theological Seminary.

It was in January of 2011 in a seminary class that God again moved in a remarkable way, directing his story and guiding his plan. A fellow seminarian invited me to dinner to meet his wife and child, and in the course of the conversation, they asked me how I had decided to become a pastor. "You would never believe it," was my answer, "but God used a most remarkable circumstance to draw me into pastoral ministry." I then began to share with the family the story of God's hand in saving my life. "Someday," I said, "I believe God wants me to write a book about this story." My friend immediately quipped, "You know I work for a book publisher, don't you?"

Well, that was the beginning of a whole new journey. As I met with the publisher, sharing the story, he spoke with deliberation, "Rose, you say you believe that Matt, too, has a story to share. We think you ought to try to contact him." The words struck a chord deep within my heart, and, surprisingly enough, I found enthusiasm rather than dread began to emerge. But I had a problem. How would I find him after all these years?

Intersection Again

Immediately I thought back to a strange and unusual encounter I had had some months earlier. On my way to a bridal shower I had stopped by the supermarket to pick up a potato salad in the deli. It was a store in a nearby town that I never frequent, and stopping by the deli was never on my usual shopping list. But this day was different. As I picked out a salad, I glanced up to see Matt's wife looking at me from the other side of the counter. My face registered shock, since I had not seen her for so many years. "Hi! How are you doing? How is Matt doing?" After a favorable answer we talked briefly, then I left for my party.

Now I knew how I would try to find Matt. But I was soon to be disappointed. His wife had moved to another deli across town. Three times I drove to the deli with the hope of catching her at work. Three times they said she was off for the day. Then one day as I was leaving the store, not seeing her behind the counter, and finding no one to inquire as to her whereabouts, I caught a brief vision of someone passing in front of a distant door. It was Matt's wife. We finally connected, and I asked her to give Matt a message that my husband and I wanted to meet with him. I didn't know at the time that this was her last day; she was quitting her job the following day. God had provided a small window for our paths to cross again.

Three days later, on the Friday before Easter, the four of us set up a time to meet in a Village Inn in Fort Collins. Matt picked the spot. Interesting that it was in the same restaurant chain in which he had been arrested fifteen and a half years earlier. I wasn't sure what to expect or how my heart would handle it all, I just knew I needed to do this. It was an overcast day as we opened the door to the restaurant and scanned the tables for Matt and his wife. I glanced at my husband, thankful that Steve was here with me. My heart was beating faster than normal as anticipation and trepidation stirred together an unusual concoction in my stomach. Since it had been so long since we had seen each other, I didn't know if I would recognize them. Finally my eyes landed on a table in the distance, and I knew they had come. The man sitting there had a face I recognized, but his hair was pulled back in a ponytail and had grown long, and gray had set in. When we approached, Matt looked down, his head hung, almost in a look of shame and guilt. What must he be thinking? Was he expecting anger? Rebuke? A good tongue-lashing?

My heart flooded with compassion. This man had gone through so much. Now he was here to meet with me at my request. Breaking the ice was the only thing to do. I reached down and gave him and his wife each a hug. "How are you?" "It is so good to see you!" It didn't take long before the floodgates opened. "Rose, all these years I thought I had ruined your life," Matt said softly.

"No, just the opposite happened! I wouldn't want to go through it again, but, Matt, I wouldn't change what happened for anything," I answered. We wept together as we shared the journey of our lives and God's incredible intervention through it all. Matt looked at me with tears filling his eyes and said, "I am so sorry for all that I've put you through. Will you forgive me?" "Matt," I said, "Yes, I forgive you. I forgave you long ago. God has taken all that has happened and brought so much good out of it. You don't owe me anything. I am just grateful." More tears.

It was my husband's turn to speak, and the words that came out of his mouth caused me to utter a slight gasp. "Matt, would you and your wife like to come over to our home and talk some more?" A week later they came to our house, walked up to the front door, climbing the same steps that had been the pathway to potential destruction sixteen years earlier. The last time Matt had ascended them, he had a lethal weapon concealed in his pocket and foreboding motives were clouding his thoughts. The last time he had entered through this doorway, he was on a rapid course to self-destruction, and he probably would have taken me with him. How could things now be so different? Only because of God.

Sitting in my living room that day, I finally got to hear the rest of the story. How often are we granted this luxury? How had the tapes inexplicably shown up on the kitchen counter long ago? After sixteen years the mystery was revealed. Matt had come to the house three months earlier with sinister intentions, hoping to use the excuse of returning the Christian tapes we had given him to get entrance into the house. Steve's mother answered the door and explained that she was watching the boys for a few days while we were out of town. Matt realized his intended target was gone, so he handed her the tapes and left. None of us were any the wiser of how close our children had come to sheer disaster, or how near they had been to malicious evil while we were away. I wondered how often I was oblivious to other stories that only God could see. Surely he is protecting us more than we ever realize.

Suddenly Matt turned his attention to the area in front of the stereo and fixed his eyes on the spot, becoming strangely silent. It was as if he was coming to grips with this place of torment so many years ago. Finally he turned to me and said, "Rose, you could have said a lot of things, but when you started to pray, everything changed. When you began praying it was like you had the strength of Goliath, and I became helpless and weak. I couldn't move to hurt you." It was as if the memories came flooding back in such a rapid-fire manner that it was hard to contain. He continued, "And Rose, when you were at the front door, it was as if the door just blew open. I know that God let you out of the house." The conversation continued in a similar fashion as Matt recalled detail after detail of the near fatal day.

In a strange way, this dialogue was a part of the healing for both of us, and our spouses. We had come full circle and could see a providential hand in the darkest and most devastating experiences of our lives. It was a joy for all of us to see things in a new way. We had the church send a CD to Matt, which was the message in 1997 of me telling the full story with every detail. He had listened to it before he came. His words still astound me. "This story is picture-perfect of what I remember. Usually it is 'his story' and 'her story,' and the true reality is somewhere in the middle. But every detail you spoke about is exactly as I remember." How uncanny. Both of us were able to remember minute details about a day sixteen years ago as if it were yesterday. And the details concurred.

Then Matt looked at me and said, "You know, you said something to me on the curb just before I left that wasn't on the CD. Do you remember what you said?" I looked back blankly. "Rose, you looked right at me and said, 'And I never want to see you back here at my house again.' Then you paused for a moment, looked up at me and said, 'I'm going to amend that. I never want to see you back here at my house with these intentions.'"

I remembered it well. While sitting on the curb that day long ago in 1995, I had a flashing picture run through my brain in just a matter of seconds. It was so strange that I only shared it with a few others. It was a picture of Matt and his wife sitting in our living room some time in the future. Woven into the visual image was the impression that there had been restoration and a spiritual awakening of some sort. It was a picture that I had carried close to my heart for sixteen years when I had known that God was not finished working with Matt. The fleeting image had given me hope all this time that Matt would find healing and new life in

Jesus Christ. It was a passing vision that had made me confident throughout the years that the story was still being written and that Matt would have a testimony to tell of the faithfulness and goodness of God. I remembered well that the mental image had passed through my mind between those two sentences. "Yes, Matt, I remember saying that," I said, and shared the picture that had invaded my thinking for only but a brief moment. "It is why I amended what I said. I knew that someday you would be back in my home under totally different circumstances." The preview that God had given that day, sixteen years earlier, had come true. Matt and his wife were here in our living room—the same room where he had held me at knifepoint years ago. The same room where evil had been intended, but good had been brought about instead. We had come full circle and God was to be given the glory.

Over the next two years the story continued to unfold. The dimensions of grace interlaced throughout each of our journeys brought a myriad of emotions—sometimes repulsion at the realization of how things could have turned out, sometimes tears of angst at the realities of the pain, sometimes laughter at the absurdities that now appeared so obvious, but mostly overflowing gratitude at the radical faithfulness of God, and knee-bending awe at the magnitude and grandeur of his love.

CHAPTER THIRTEEN

Victim No More

Who Am I?

Our identities had been altered at the core. When I was incarcerated in a shadowy and gloomy prison cell, my own sense of worthlessness and the dismal failure of my life preoccupied me day and night. Who was I, really? A rapist? An assailant? Could I ever be trusted again? Why would anyone want to be in my company? I saw myself as one who had little value and a man destined to be discarded and abandoned. I felt I had destroyed the life of another human being and probably destroyed her whole family as well. I deserved retaliation, revenge, and ruthless punishment. Underneath my emotionless exterior lay a man without hope and without identity other than the one I had acted out—a socially deviant criminal. The courts had confirmed my identity. I was a felon, a convict, a sex offender. I already had the label pasted across my green prison garb in the form of my official prison number; I might as well have it pasted across my forehead. Everyone knew what I was. I couldn't run or deny it. Might as well accept the inevitable and live up to expectations.

But something changed the night I surrendered my life to Christ. Something washed over me that was hard to explain. In that moment of time a heavy blow was dealt to the identity that I had accepted for most of my life. In a small but significant way I caught a glimpse of a new and surprising reality. God had communicated with me. Maybe God wasn't rejecting me. Maybe God wasn't discarding me in anger. There was a sense that I had been forgiven and was being drawn to a new place, a place of belonging, a place of acceptance. It was hard to grasp at first but the truth began to seep into my being little by little until, by an inexplicable act of redemption, it broke into my shattered heart and began to take root. I was loved. I was desired. I was not a rapist; I was a son. A son of God.

This essential transformation at the center of my identity produced a miracle. Yes, I had failed and acted out in a devastating, evil, and destructive manner. But that was not my identity. My new position as a child of God was my real distinctive. Now I could begin to be the new man I knew that I was called to be—my true self. Throughout the months and years that followed, this true reality took over the old labels of shame that I had worn all my life. I could begin to hold my head high. I knew who I was. I was forgiven, adopted, changed, and made whole by the one who loved me. That one was my Father above. Scriptures confirmed in powerful words what was awakening deep in my soul, "See what great love the Father has lavished on us, that we should be called children of God! And that is what we are!"[32] The miracle began when I understood who I truly was because of the great love of Jesus Christ. A beloved son. The miracle continues as I learn to live in this new identity and understand my new standing with God. The radical change that took place in me is rooted here.

Another thing that changed my perspective was learning how to forgive myself. I knew I had to accept responsibility for what I had done and admit my shortcomings rather than hide from them. I confessed to God and knew I was forgiven, but I think it took a while to really feel forgiven. It is such a hard concept to get. Something inside of me wanted to pay God back for the wrongs in my life. How was I to accept forgiveness without a charge? Didn't I have to work hard to prove myself? But slowly God broke through with his message of love. I wasn't forgiven because I earned it or deserved it. I didn't receive his pardon because I worked hard enough and paid him back. It was a gift. It was a gift he was giving because of who he is—a God of incredible mercy, compassion, and love. He was asking me to confess my sins to him and turn away from them in another direction. Then he did something for me that I could never do for myself. He paid my debt. Jesus had paid it all on a cross. It was his gift of love. The overwhelming truth of this fact took some time to soak into my weary heart. But slowly it did. If a holy and perfect God forgave me, why can't I forgive me? The more I allowed my heart to be open to his love and forgiveness, the more I began to forgive myself.

Oh, I still realize how repugnant and offensive my sin is. A holy God died so he could take me out of that place, and he never wants me to have to go back there. My sin cost him a lot. It cost him everything. Now he invites me to his forgiveness and healing. My shame turned to gratitude, my broken life became new, and my wounded soul found love. Out of this place my new life flows.

There are things I have put into my life today, not because I feel obligated or forced, but because I choose to out of sheer gratitude. I meet on a regular basis with my pastor who is providing me with wise counsel, guidance, and accountability. He has helped and encouraged me more than I can ever describe. I also make it a regular habit to be at my wife's side in church. It is more than supporting her. I am growing, learning, and becoming more and more who God wants me to be. I was once caught up in something much bigger than me, and I never want to go back there. I appreciate too much where I've come. My joy is real, and my sense of being alive inside isn't worth trading for anything.

Today I am not ashamed of me. I'm a different person. I like myself and enjoy my own company now. I trust myself with myself. I don't have to prove myself or try to feel better by destructive behavior. I'm not a person who hurts others. When people see me they see a good man who is filled with compassion and caring for others. They see a man of personal integrity, a hard worker, and one who loves his wife and children. They see a person who is accountable, honest, and a man of his word. They see a selfless guy who would help anybody. Today I know who I am, I know who God is, and I know what's important in life.

Prison teaches you to value things that you took for granted before. Like a heart that is at peace and free. It is hard to express how much I treasure this gift from God. In all honesty, no one knows the relief better than I do. I know I can never repay God for what he has done, but I can embrace the gift, enjoy the gift, cherish the gift, and live my life in gratitude. Today I am aware that the transformation in me was not a drug or a high-tech treatment. It was God. I don't know all the ways he did it. I just know the credit goes to him.

Or do you show contempt for the riches of his kindness, forbearance and patience, not realizing that God's kindness is intended to lead you to repentance?—Romans 2:4

Thanks be to God for his indescribable gift!
—2 Corinthians 9:15

Labeled Victim

I too, had an identity adjustment to make. The courts had regularly referred to me as a "victim." In truth I had been a victim of a crime. But was this to be my self-description? Was I from here on out going to be labeled as a helpless person, someone who had experienced harm and was now powerless to do anything about it? Was this who I really was? These questions propelled me on a journey that led to a new place of discovery. I began to see myself in a new identity, which allowed me to become aware of the pitfalls of seeing myself as a victim. Out of this place God was able to confront my fear and release me from its strangling effects.

It is interesting to note that when you Google the word "victim," you end up with thousands of sites. It is a word that is central to the dialogue of our culture. There are a myriad of things one may fall victim to, and an abundance of resources where one may find support in victimization. There is nothing wrong with support for victims; in fact it is a good thing to champion the cause of those who have been mistreated and abused, and to provide resources for recovery. Scripture admonishes us to "defend the weak and the fatherless; uphold the cause of the poor and the oppressed."[33] God himself takes on this role with vigor. Another psalm says, "But you, God, see the trouble of the afflicted; you consider their grief and take it in hand. The victims commit themselves to you; you are the helper of the fatherless."[34] God truly has a heart for those who have been victimized, and he comes to the rescue in help and healing.

However, I realized that when the role of "victim" becomes the identity that I absorb and live out, it can be debilitating and paralyzing. It can also be a source of great fear. I can begin to think I am helpless and at the mercy of others more powerful. This isn't what God has for me. I was surprised when I saw that the King James Version of the Bible never used the word "victim" because there is no direct Hebrew or Greek equivalent. My exploration revealed that the New International Version, a much loved translation, uses the word "victim" only sixteen times with all but one usage being in the Old Testament. In each case the word is used when translating Hebrew words meaning "slain," "prey," or an "unhappy or unfortunate person." As I searched through Scripture, I found no place where the word "victim" is used to describe the identity of a believer in God.

It was with this discovery that I realized I had to change my thinking. While I had been the recipient of the hurtful and detrimental actions of another human being, I was not, at my core, a victim. I noticed that many godly people of the Bible knew first-hand what difficulty, abuse, ridicule and oppression meant. Paul was shipwrecked, David was hunted, Jeremiah was beaten and imprisoned, Elisha was slandered, and Stephen was stoned. Most had experienced a lot worse than I had. God had another message of identity he wanted me to understand, and it was one that would impact me greatly.

Then my eyes fell on a story in Scripture. It was the story of Christ himself. Tears welled as God broke through the barriers of my heart with a fresh revelation of his own suffering. In just two chapters of Matthew, Jesus is plotted against, betrayed by a disciple, abandoned by a friend, stripped, mocked, abused, beaten, and ultimately nailed, bruised and bleeding, to a wooden cross. His greatest agony seemed to come when it appeared that even God his Father had abandoned him.[35] As I thought about this, I noticed that nowhere did Scripture call Jesus a "victim." Even in the darkest of his hours, he seemed to move forward with an identity firmly planted within his very being. That identity was not a helpless victim.

A new understanding came that would be instrumental in my own healing. I too could refuse to be labeled as a victim. I too could choose to embrace a different identity. It was true that I was powerless in my own strength, but there was power in God's strength. This change of thinking seemed to confront fear head-on. I realized how easy it would be to succumb to fear's paralyzing effects.

I also came across a Scripture that seemed to unlock my understanding like a new clue in a grand treasure hunt. "But thanks be to God! He gives us the victory through our Lord Jesus Christ."[36] Jesus was giving me the opportunity to be a victor rather than a victim! I found the context of this verse remarkable. It is a chapter talking about the truth of the resurrection. All the suffering that Jesus went through did not end in defeat. It ended in victory! He rose from the dead! The Scripture told me that since he was raised from the dead as our forerunner, all those whose faith is in him will rise again to new life too. That meant that even my greatest enemy—even death—is also defeated by Jesus Christ. That day I knew that nothing could come against me that had not already been overcome by the death and resurrection of Jesus. I was not a victim, even if Matt had taken my life. I was a victor through Christ.

As I contemplated this new identity, things began to change on the inside. I saw myself in a new way. Instead of thinking "I can't," I began to focus on Scriptures that said, "I can" through Christ. "I can do all this through him who gives me strength."[37] Instead of being defined by life's circumstances, I began to let myself be defined by the Word of God.

His child. His beloved. His daughter. Called by his name. Victorious in him. All these messages began to take root and grow into a sturdy, stable, and immovable oak within the recesses of my heart. I believed God's promises. He wasn't going to let me go. What he had begun, he would bring to completion. I could trust him even when I couldn't see the evidence of what I hoped for with my own eyes.

Yes, the courts had called me a victim and rightly so. Yet I realized this didn't have to be my identity, and I didn't have to stay in this place. I had been the recipient of a crime, but I could choose how to see it. I could choose to see it as an opportunity for God to show his faithfulness and power on my behalf. I could choose to see it as a time when I was loved. Through it all I could say, "Thanks be to God! He gives victory through our Lord Jesus Christ."

And we know that in all things God works for the good of those who love him, who have been called according to his purpose.—Romans 8:28

CHAPTER FOURTEEN

And One Thing Remains

This is my love story. Granted, it is probably a different kind of love story than you have read before. But it is a love story nonetheless. It is a story of the radical, redemptive, tenacious, abundant, unfailing, overwhelming, satisfying, life-changing love of God. It is a love that gave up his life to rescue us. It is a love that goes to the ends of the earth to save us. It is a love that went to hell and back to redeem us. It is a love that poured out all of heaven to draw us to himself. It is a love that suffered so that he may adopt us as sons and daughters, call us by his name, and bring us into his own family. It is a love that sacrificed all so that he could have us with him throughout eternity.

Matt's life and my life were transformed by this love. The truth is, we are both in the same place, sinners saved by grace. We both experienced healing from his hand. We both revel in forgiveness and the "paid in full" stamp that was placed on our debt. We both found our fears melted and our wounds restored. We both saw how God was able to take the evil that was intended by the enemy and use it for good. We both experienced the hand of God in plucking us from the pit and giving us new life and a fresh start.

It is reminiscent of the biblical story of Lazarus. Jesus spoke powerful words, then brought them to life with a demonstration.

He said, "I am the resurrection and the life. The one who believes in me will live, even though they die; and whoever lives by believing in me will never die. Do you believe this?" Moments later he uttered the words, "Lazarus, come out!" and a man dead four days emerged from the tomb, made whole by the Giver of Life.[38] This event gave resurrection hope to believers for millennia to follow, and the story has been quoted every century since it was first told. And rightly so. Yet there is also a terrestrial application. Jesus is in the resurrection business right here, right now, on this side of death. He is pulling those dead in sin, bound in addiction, and incapacitated in fear out of the place of darkness and breathing in hope, breakthrough, healing, and life. He truly is the resurrection and the life. Both Matt and I say, "God saved my life," and mean it.

Yes, each of us knows we haven't arrived. Life is a journey, and we continue to grow and learn until we say our final goodbye. But it is a journey that is undergirded by strength, it is infused with hope, it is held in peace, and it is secured by love. Challenges still come, and pitfalls still appear in the road. Struggles continue, and hardships plague us from time to time. But we know who we are, we know who God is, and we know what's important in life. He has a purpose and plan, and he will faithfully bring it to conclusion. He just asks that we stay surrendered to his will, humbled before him, and faithful to him. It is his job to continue the work of transformation. "And so we are transfigured much like the Messiah, our lives gradually becoming brighter and more beautiful as God enters our lives and we become like him."[39]

It all really boils down to love. God's love. He has written it in the sky, he has spelled it out in his Word, and he has painted it in blood on an ugly wooden cross. His message is love. The Apostle John gave us a Scripture, which has become well known, that points to the cross as the ultimate symbol of love: "For God so loved the world that he gave his one and only Son, that whoever believes in him shall not perish but have eternal life."[40] Writing later in a letter, he wrote something similar: "This is how we know what love is: Jesus Christ laid down his life for us. And we ought to lay down our lives for our brothers and sisters."[41]

The Apostle Paul knew love. In his earlier days as an archenemy of Jesus, he persecuted anyone who claimed to follow his Name. But then he had an encounter with the one he sought to defeat. The encounter changed his life, and he became one of the greatest champions of the gospel that the world has ever known. Here are his words:

> *"So, what do you think? With God on our side like this, how can we lose? If God didn't hesitate to put everything on the line for us, embracing our condition and exposing himself to the worst by sending his own Son, is there anything else he wouldn't gladly and freely do for us? And who would dare tangle with God by messing with one of God's chosen? Who would dare even to point a finger? The One who died for us—who was raised to life for us!—is in the presence of God at this very moment sticking up for us. Do you think anyone is going to be able to drive a wedge between us and Christ's love for us? There is no way! Not trouble, not hard times, not hatred, not hunger, not homelessness, not bullying threats, not backstabbing, not even the worst sins listed in Scripture:*
>
> > *They kill us in cold blood because they hate you.*
> > *We're sitting ducks; they pick us off one by one.*
> > *None of this fazes us because Jesus loves us. I'm absolutely convinced that nothing—nothing living or*

> *dead, angelic or demonic, today or tomorrow, high or*
> *low, thinkable or unthinkable—absolutely nothing can*
> *get between us and God's love because of the way that*
> *Jesus our Master has embraced us.*[42]

Yes, the cross is the supreme symbol of love. Perfect love. The good news is that perfect love flowed into ultimate victory. Jesus rose from the dead in power and glory to establish his kingdom. It is a kingdom that was inaugurated at the cross, and its consummation is yet to be. It is a kingdom where violence will be eliminated and peace restored. It is a kingdom where all tears will be wiped away and loved ones will be reunited. It is a kingdom free from evil, where justice prevails, where truth permeates, and where joy abounds. The kingdom that Jesus came to establish gathers his people together from every nation, language, and people group. The kingdom yet to come is one of righteousness, healing, and unity. It is a kingdom where Jesus Christ is king. Maybe he is even wearing his crown of stars plucked from the Corona Borealis. It is a kingdom of *love*. Love will be the law of the land.

The kingdom of God is yet to fully come on earth, but we see evidence of its breaking in now. We get to experience a taste of it here. There is kingdom activity all around. You can see it where love flows. *Love*. It is what will see us through. It is the power that will take us to the desired end. It is what really matters. And after all is sifted through, when all is stripped away, when all is shaken down, and when all is settled out, it is love that remains. Because God is *love*.

Notes

Chapter 3: Aftermath of Emotion

1. Job 35:10.
2. Psalm 42:8.
3. Michael Ledner, "You Are My Hiding Place" (Universal Music-Brentwood-Benson Publishing/CCM Music, 1981).

Chapter 4: Navigating the Fallout

4. 2 Kings 18–19.
5. Psalm 46.
6. Psalm 27.

Chapter 5: Power of God in the Public Sector

7. Steve Camp, "Love That Will Not Let Me Go," from the "Justice" album (Sparrow Records: Universal Music Group, 1988).

Chapter 6: Release from Fear

8. Elisabeth Elliott, *Keep a Quiet Heart* (Ada, MI: Baker, 2004).
9. Genesis 50:20.
10. John 14:27.
11. John 14:1.
12. 1 John 4:18.
13. Matthew 8:23–27.
14. Philippians 4:8.
15. Philippians 4:6–7.
16. Hebrews 13:5–6.

Chapter 8: Freedom of Forgiveness

17. 1 John 1:9.
18. Romans 12:17–19.
19. Philip Yancey, *What's So Amazing About Grace?* (Grand Rapids: Zondervan, 1997), 98.

20. Yancy, 99.
21. Yancy, 100.
22. Luke 23:34.
23. Isaiah 30:15.
24. Psalm 103:11–13.

Chapter 10: Awakened by Love

25. Deuteronomy 1:31.
26. Ephesians 2:4.
27. Henry Scougal, *The Life of God in the Soul of Man* (London: T. Pridden, 1776), 61.
28. John 12:1–8.
29. Jeremiah 29:13–14.
30. Philippians 3:8.
31. Romans 8:38–39.

Chapter 13: Victim No More

32. 1 John 3:1.
33. Psalm 82:3.
34. Psalm 10:14.
35. Matthew 26–27.
36. 1 Corinthians 15:57.
37. Philippians 4:13.

Chapter 14: And One Thing Remains

38. John 11:17–44.
39. 2 Corinthians 3:18. Eugene Peterson, *The Message* (Colorado Springs: Navpress, 1994), 373.
40. John 3:16.
41. 1 John 3:16.
42. Romans 8:31–39. Peterson, 320.

Acknowledgments

Gratitude is what characterizes all I feel. There have been so many people who have supported, encouraged, and prayed into this story over the last seventeen and a half years. I could never thank you all, but you have made a profound impact and been a part of what God is doing to reveal himself to humanity. Thank you.

Thank you to the wonderful pastors and staff of Grace Place Church who have been a part of nurturing this story for many years. Working with you for almost fourteen years has taught me more than you will ever know of God's love and grace. Special thanks to Clay Peck, Steve Kurtright, Brenda Pearson, Cheri Scott, Melody Sumner, Mark Johnson, Gregg Chaddic, Sue Sermersheim, Michael Butts, Kathy Ross, Kim Land, Jamie and Tiffany Degnan, and Dave Lawson.

Thank you to the Mill City Church family and staff who have poured life, prayer, encouragement, and love into my life and this book-writing project. You are a gift from God to me. Special thanks to Aaron and Jossie Stern, Justin Steinhart, Grant and Carly Barron, Wes and Jo Tongue, Kevin and Heather Deese, Nick and Hilary Tompkins, and Beau and Nicole Johnson.

Thank you to Joyce Druchunas, Jon Mitchell, Cheri Scott, and Sue and Dan Sermersheim. The years that we met to pray weekly continues to be a reservoir from which I draw regularly. Thank you for your love.

Thank you to my treasured friends with Ethan Henry Publishing Services, Volney and Karen James. You were the first publishers to believe in this story, and this book would not be possible without your invaluable help, support, encouragement, and wisdom. Thank you also to Erica Pauly, Karen James, Michaela Dodd, John Dunham, Michael Simonov, and Bekah Thrasher for your conscientious editing, creative ideas, and valuable input. I am awed by your love for Jesus and for the capable and God-inspired way you helped shape the story.

Thank you to Matt for your willingness to be interviewed for long hours and to vulnerably share your story for the enrichment and good of others. I am awed at what God has done in your life.

Thank you to my amazing parents, Marilyn and Alvin Thunquest. You have taught me the things of God from my childhood by your example and love. Thank you to my mother-in-law, Loneta Pauly, my faithful husband of thirty-five years, Steve Pauly, and my sons, Brent, Chris, and Ryan, and daughter-in-law, Erica. This book would have never been possible without your strength, encouragement, and love. I love you all dearly.

Most importantly, thank you to God who saved my life on that day seventeen and a half years ago and most significantly, for eternity. Thank you for giving me the words to write your story.